Learn Span Beginners In Y While You Sleep: Language Learning To Intermediate Levels- Grammar, 1000+ Phrases & Conversation Skills+ Short Spanish Bedtime Stories For Adults

Table of Contents

Why Learning Spanish Is A Good Idea

Learning a new language can open up countless opportunities you never imagined. Wether it be new friendships, job positions, or romantic relationships, learning a new language allows you to hack life itself, granting you access to people and experiences worth living. Additionally, Spanish is one of the world's most spoken languages, so learning to speak the tongue will bridge you to new cultures and countries like Brazil and the amazing Amazon forest engulfing it, Argentina and the delicious meat they offer, Peru with their traditional ceviche, or perhaps a relaxing vacation in the Caribbean, zipping "piña coladas," while your skin tans under the warm tropical sun.

This book will serve as a tool that will help you learn Spanish fast and easy. You can learn Spanish in your car and even while you sleep. Our breakdown will be pretty dynamic, so there will be a lot of participation from you in the process. The more you practice, the faster you'll learn.

We are breaking down this book into twelve different parts, all tackling a different branch of conversation in the Spanish language. You will learn new words and phrases you can then implement in real-life situations or practice with a friend. The idea o give you a learning experience as pure as sible, very divorced from the traditional proaches that take ages to learn.

e will go over introductory phrases, travel, food & estaurants, animals, friendship & conversation, ews & sports, romance, business, politics, entertainment, job interviews, and family. Each chapter will contain a combination of words and phrases, followed by stories written in English and Spanish, and a final chapter test to prove your skills. Feel free to go over each chapter until you fully master every word. Practice makes perfect.

Part One: Introductory Phrases

Welcome to chapter one of your Spanish learning experience. We will be focusing on introductory words and phrases. The first part of learning any language is learning how to first introduce yourself to strangers. An introduction is the first experience you'll ever have, so we better prepare you well. This chapter contains over 80 phrases, so be sure to practice both context, definition, and pronunciation, before you skip ahead. Answers to the test at the end of the chapter will be available as footnotes.

English: Hello, my name is Pedro.

Spanish: Hola, mi nombre es Pedro.

—

English: Good morning, how are you today?

Spanish: Buenos días, ¿cómo te encuentras hoy?

—

English: Good afternoon, what is your name?

Spanish: Buenas tardes, ¿cómo te llamas?

—

English: Good morning, Pedro, how are you feeling today? Do you happen to know what time is it?

Spanish: Buenos días, Pedro ¿cómo te encuentras hoy? ¿Sabes qué hora es?

—

English: Hello sir, my name is Pedro, what is your name?

Spanish: Hola señor, mi nombre es Pedro ¿cuál es tu nombre?

—

English: Excuse me sir, what time is it?

Spanish: Disculpe señor ¿qué hora es?

—

English: Excuse me sir, do you know what day is it?

Spanish: Disculpe señor ¿sabe qué día es?

—

English: Hello everyone! My name is Pedro.

Spanish: ¡Hola a todos! Mi nombre es Pedro.

—

English: Excuse me lady ¿would you tell me your name?

Spanish: Disculpa señorita ¿me podrías decir tu nombre?

—

English: Hello Julia, it is a pleasure to meet you.

Spanish: Hola Julia, un placer en conocerte.

—

English: The pleasure is all mine.

Spanish: El placer es todo mío.

—

English: Excuse me sir, do you speak Spanish?

Spanish: Disculpa señor ¿usted habla Español?

—

English: Excuse me miss, do you know where is the nearest coffee shop?

Spanish: Disculpe señorita ¿sabes dónde queda la tienda de café más cercana?

—

English: My name is Jose and I'm from Puerto Rico. Where are you from?

Spanish: Mi nombre es Jose y soy de Puerto Rico. ¿De dónde tú eres?

—

English: In my country, most people speak Spanish.

Spanish: En mi país, la mayoría de las personas hablan Español.

—

English: Nice to see you again Pedro, it is always nice to see a friend.

Spanish: Qué bueno verte de nuevo Pedro, siempre es agradable ver a un amigo.

—

English: Pedro is from Puerto Rico so he probably knows how to speak both English and Spanish.

Spanish: Pedro es de Puerto Rico, así que probablemente sepa hablar tanto Inglés como Español.

—

English: Jose and Laura are full siblings, they share both parents.

Spanish: Jose y Laura son hermanos, comparten ambos padres.

—

English: Hello, my name is Manuel and I'm not from around here.

Spanish: Hola, mi nombre es Manuel y no soy de aquí.

—

English: Hello, my name is Manuel and I'm a student.

Spanish: Hola, mi nombre es Manuel y soy un estudiante.

—

English: Welcome to the country, hope you have a great time.

Spanish: Bienvenido al país, espero tengas un excelente tiempo aquí.

—

English: Maria knows Jose. They went to school together.

Spanish: Maria conoce a José. Fueron a la escuela juntos.

—

English: Hello Manuel, this is Pedro, my friend from Uruguay.

Spanish: Hola Manuel, este es Pedro, mi amigo de Uruguay.

—

English: Nice to meet you, Pedro. I've never been to Uruguay.

Spanish: Un placer en conocerte, Pedro. Nunca he ido a Uruguay.

—

English: Do you speak Spanish?

Spanish: ¿Hablas Español?

—

English: I do not speak Spanish.

Spanish: No hablo Español.

—

English: I do not speak Spanish, but I'm learning.

Spanish: Yo no hablo Español, pero estoy aprendiendo.

—

English: Be careful driving.

Spanish: Ten cuidado conduciendo.

—

English: Good luck!

Spanish: ¡Buena suerte!

—

English: Hello Manuel, are you feeling okay?

Spanish: Hola Manuel ¿te sientes bien?

—

English: Don't worry, I'm feeling very good.

Spanish: No te preocupes, me siento muy bien.

—

English: Do you know where the school is?

Spanish: ¿Sabes dónde queda la escuela?

—

English: My father is friends with yours.

Spanish: Mi padre es amigo del tuyo.

—

English: My sister knows Laura, they go to school together.

Spanish: Mi hermana conoce a Laura, van a la escuela juntas.

—

English: Hello, I'm new in town and don't have any friends. Would you like to be my friend?

Spanish: Hola, soy nuevo en el pueblo y no tengo amigos. ¿Te gustaría ser mi amigo?

—

English: What are you doing today?

Spanish: ¿Qué vas a hacer hoy?

—

English: What plans do you have for the weekend?

Spanish: ¿Que planes tienes para el fin de semana?

—

English: My name is Joseph and I don't like sports.

Spanish: Mi nombre es Joseph y no me gustan los deportes.

—

English: I do not know where the school is.

Spanish: No sé dónde queda la escuela.

—

English: I don't know where the school is, but I can help you find it.

Spanish: Yo no sé dónde queda la escuela, pero puedo ayudarte a encontrarla.

—

English: What do you want to do today?

Spanish: ¿Qué quieres hacer hoy?

—

English: My name is Pedro and I'm 23-years-old.

Spanish: Mi nombre es Pedro y tengo 23 años.

—

English: Teenagers usually have between thirteen and twenty years of age.

Spanish: Los adolescentes tienen entre trece y veinte años de edad.

—

English: My sister is eleven years old.

Spanish: Mi hermana tiene once años.

—

English: I have two younger brothers. Pedro is four, while Martin is two.

Spanish: Tengo dos hermanos menores. Pedro tiene cuatro, mientras Martin tiene dos.

—

English: It is a great day today, perfect to go fishing.

Spanish: Hoy es un gran día, perfecto para ir de pesca.

—

English: The night is very cold, perhaps we should go inside.

Spanish: La noche está muy fría, sería bueno ir dentro.

—

English: Tonight is perfect to go out and grab something to drink.

Spanish: Esta noche es perfecta para salir por algo de comer.

—

English: Tell Maria and Juan that we will be going out tonight.

Spanish: Dile a Maria y Juan que vamos a salir esta noche.

—

English: Emily won't be coming home tonight, she will be studying all night at Vilma's house.

Spanish: Emily no vendrá a casa esta noche, estará estudiando toda la noche en casa de Vilma.

—

English: There will always be a next time.

Spanish: Siempre habrá una próxima vez.

—

English: Good morning, time to wake up and have some fun under the sun.

Spanish: Buen día, es tiempo de despertarse y disfrutar debajo del sol.

—

English: How did you sleep last night?

Spanish: ¿Cómo dormiste anoche?

—

English: I had a terrible night, yesterday.

Spanish: Ayer tuve una noche terrible.

—

English: I failed the test.

Spanish: No aprobé el examen.

—

English: I aced the test.

Spanish: Aprobé el examen.

—

English: The shop is not very far from where we are.

Spanish: La tienda no queda muy lejos de donde estamos.

—

English: We are getting closer.

Spanish: Nos estamos acercando.

—

English: The shop is near.

Spanish: La tienda esta cerca.

—

English: Pedro lives far away from his school. He has to wake up early to arrive on time.

Spanish: Pedro vive muy lejos de la escuela. Él tiene que despertarse temprano cada mañana para llegar a tiempo.

—

English: Maria lives close to the school. She can even walk there if she wants.

Spanish: Maria vive cerca de la escuela. Incluso, ella puede caminar hasta allí si quiere.

—

English: We are both walking to the school today.

Spanish: Ambos estamos caminando a la escuela hoy.

—

English: Hello Jim! Do you want to walk home with me?

Spanish: Hola Jim! ¿Quieres caminar a casa conmigo?

—

English: I'd love to help you.

Spanish: Me encantaría ayudarte.

—

English: Sorry, can't right now.

Spanish: Perdón, no puedo ahora mismo.

—

English: I'm so sorry, don't have time.

Spanish: Perdón, no tengo tiempo.

—

English: Maybe next time.

Spanish: Tal vez la próxima.

—

English: I'm aware we don't know each other.

Spanish: Estoy consciente que no nos conocemos.

—

English: I don't feel good.

Spanish: No me siento bien.

—

English: Congratulations, that was very good!

Spanish: Felicidades, ¡eso estuvo muy bien!

—

English: Pedro is a very talented student. He also plays baseball on weekends.

Spanish: Pedro es un estudiante muy talentoso. También juega béisbol los fines de semana.

—

English: Amazing! How did you do that?

Spanish: ¡Increíble! ¿Cómo hiciste eso?

—

English: That is very impressive!

Spanish: ¡Eso es muy impresionante!

—

English: I'm confident we are on the right track.

Spanish: Estoy confiado que estamos en el camino correcto.

—

English: I'm not sure.

Spanish: No estoy seguro.

—

English: Don't tell me you don't know where you're going?

Spanish: No me digas que no sabes a dónde vas.

—

English: Meeting new people is always fun.

Spanish: Conocer gente nueva siempre es divertido.

—

English: Our friends will introduce us to their new group of friends.

Spanish: Nuestros amigos nos van a presentar a sus amigos.

—

English: We are all excited to meet you.

Spanish: Todos estamos emocionados de conocerte.

—

English: There is no need to apologize, hope to see you next time!

Spanish: No hay necesidad de disculparte ¡espero verte la próxima vez!

—

STORY-TIME Chapter 1: Pedro The New Student (English)

Pedro is from Puerto Rico but he lives in Miami. He moved there last month with his family. He is the new student in his school and is having a hard time making new friends. Pedro is very shy and does not speak English very well. However, one lucky day, a girl approached him and introduced herself:

Maria: Hello Pedro, my name is Maria, nice to meet you!

Pedro: Hello Maria, my name is Pedro. I do not speak English.

Maria: Don't worry, I will teach you!

Pedro: That is very nice!

Maria and Pedro became good friends. Pedro went to her house every afternoon to learn English and, in turn, he taught her Spanish as well. Six months later, Pedro learned English and became very popular in class. He now has many friends and Maria to thank for that.

STORY-TIME Chapter 1: Pedro El Nuevo Estudiante (Español)

Pedro es de Puerto Rico pero vive en Miami. Se mudó con su familia hace un mes. Es el nuevo estudiante en su escuela y tiene muchos problemas en hacer nuevos amigos. Pedro es muy tímido y no habla muy bien el Inglés. Sin embargo, un día de suerte, una chica se le acercó y se presentó:

Maria: Hola Pedro, mi nombre es Maria ¡encantada de conocerte!

Pedro: ¡Hola Maria! Mi nombre es Pedro. No hablo Inglés.

Maria: ¡No te preocupes, yo te enseño!
Pedro: ¡Eso está muy bien!

Maria y Pedro se hicieron muy buenos amigos. Pedro visitaba su casa cada tarde para aprender Inglés y ella, a su vez, aprende Español de Pedro. Seis meses más tarde, Pedro aprendió Inglés y se hizo muy popular en la escuela. Ahora tiene muchos amigos y a Maria a quien agradecer por ello.

CHAPTER ONE TEST.

1 What does "buenas tardes" mean?
a) Good morning
b) Good afternoon
c) Good night
d) None of the above

2 How would you ask for someone's name in Spanish?
a) Que hora es
b) Donde queda la escuela
c) Ella es tu hermana?
d) Como te llamas?

3 How do you say goodbye in Spanish?
a) Hasta luego
b) Adiós
c) Nos vemos!
d) Todas son correctas

4 How do you ask for the time?
a) Como te llamas?
b) Que hora es?
c) Eres mi mama?
d) De dónde eres?

5 What word means far.
a) Lejos
b) Cerca
c) Dentro
d) Fuera

Answers: 1) b, 2) d, 3) d, 4) b, 5) a.

Part Two: Travel

You have aced the first chapter of our Spanish learning ebook. You can now introduce yourself to strangers and spark up some conversations. However, we all know one big reason why you're learning Spanish is because you want to travel and meet the numerous countries that speak the language. This next chapter will teach you over 80 phrases you can practice and use in real life situations, situations tailored to your travel hobby. Remember, be sure to practice.

English: I would love to travel somewhere.

Spanish: Me encantaría viajar a algún sitio.

—

English: Do you want to go on a trip with me?

Spanish: ¿Te gustaría ir a un viaje conmigo?

—

English: Sure, it would be my pleasure. Traveling is my favorite hobby.

Spanish: Claro que sí, sería un placer. Viajar es mi pasatiempo favorito.

—

English: I'm scared of boarding airplanes. I don't like heights.

Spanish: Le tengo miedo a los aviones. No me gustan las alturas.

—

English: We can go by boat, car, or airplane. Either way is fine by me.

Spanish: Podemos ir por barco, coche, o avión. Cualquier forma está bien para mí.

—

English: Have you ever traveled on a train? I hear it is a fascinating experience.

Spanish: ¿Alguna vez ha viajado en tren? He escuchado que es una experiencia fascinante.

—

English: I would love to visit every country in the planet and learn new cultures.

Spanish: Me gustaría visitar cada país en el mundo y conocer nuevas culturas.

—

English: Meet me at the airport, I bought tickets to a surprise destination.

Spanish: Nos vemos en el aeropuerto, compré boletos para ir a un destino sorpresa.

—

English: Are you bringing any luggage with you?

Spanish: ¿Traes equipaje contigo?

—

English: We should take a cab to the airport.

Spanish: Deberíamos tomar un taxi para ir al aeropuerto.

—

English: I can ask my brother to take us to the airport.

Spanish: Puedo preguntarle a mi hermano si nos puede llevar al aeropuerto.

—

English: What is our boarding time?

Spanish: ¿A que hora abordamos?

—

English: When is our flight departing?

Spanish: ¿A qué hora despega nuestro vuelo?

—

English: We should arrive early at the airport to avoid any lines.

Spanish: Si llegamos temprano al aeropuerto evitaríamos filas de espera.

—

English: Remember to read the rules of what's allowed and what's not allowed before boarding.

Spanish: Recuerda leer las reglas de que esta y que no está permitido antes de abordar.

—

English: I hope there are good movies in the airplane.

Spanish: Espero que el avión tenga buenas películas.

—

English: All I want is good food while we fly. Nothing better than that.

Spanish: Lo único que quiero es buena comida mientras volamos. No hay nada mejor que eso.

—

English: Pedro is afraid of airplanes, so he took a boat to the destination.

Spanish: Pedro le tiene miedo a los aviones, así que tomó un barco para llegar al destino.

—

English: Cruise ships are a fun alternative to travel, they have a whole world inside them.

Spanish: Los cruceros son una alternativa divertida para viajar, tienen un mundo dentro.

—

English: Are you traveling for business or leisure?

Spanish: ¿Estas viajando por negocios o placer?

—

English: I'm taking a trip to the Caribbean. The tropical weather is calling me.

Spanish: Voy a viajar al Caribe. El clima tropical me está llamando.

—

English: We must first pass airport security before we board the plane.

Spanish: Debemos pasar por migración antes de abordar.

—

English: One advantage of traveling is that you get to meet new people and experience new cultures.

Spanish: Una de las ventajas de viajar es que puedes conocer nuevas personas y experimentar nuevas culturas.

—

English: We should book a room in a good hotel before we do anything else.

Spanish: Deberíamos alquilar una habitación en un buen hotel antes que nada.

—

English: When traveling, it is always good to find a tour guide that can show you around the city.

Spanish: Al viajar, siempre es bueno buscar a un guía turístico que nos pueda enseñar la ciudad.

—

English: Traveling with friends is always better than traveling alone.

Spanish: Viajar con amigos siempre es más divertido que viajar solo.

—

English: Don't forget to take a good book when you board the plane.

Spanish: No te olvides llevar un buen libro al avión.

—

English: I slept through the whole flight.

Spanish: Dormí el vuelo completo.

—

English: The turbulence rattled the passengers on board.

Spanish: La turbulencia asustó a los pasajeros.

—

English: I can't wait until the holidays so I can finally take a break and relax on a nice vacation.

Spanish: No puedo esperar a que sean los días festivos para poder relajarme con unas buenas vacaciones.

—

English: I heard all-inclusive resorts are a very popular alternative to traveling.

Spanish: He escuchado que los hoteles todo-incluido son una alternativa muy popular al viajar.

—

English: I'm going to Miami to visit my sister. She lives there with her boyfriend.

Spanish: Me voy para Miami a visitar a mi hermana. Ella vive allá con su novio.

—

English: My boyfriend lives abroad, so we have to travel every month to see each other.

Spanish: Mi novio vive fuera, por eso viajamos cada mes para vernos.

—

English: Do you want to travel with a detailed itinerary or improvise as we go?

Spanish: ¿Prefieres viajar con un itinerario o improvisar?

—

English: What has been the most beautiful place you've visited?

Spanish: ¿Cuál ha sido el lugar más hermoso que ha visitado?

—

English: I loved traveling to the mountains. I got to see some incredible views and cold, white snow.

Spanish: Me encantó viajar a las montañas. Logré ver unos paisajes increíbles y la fría, blanca nieve.

—

English: The pandemic closed all airport travels and people could no longer experience the joy of flying.

Spanish: La pandemia cerró todos los aeropuertos y las personas ya no podían disfrutar la emoción de viajar.

—

English: After the pandemic, more people will travel.

Spanish: Después de la pandemia, más personas van a viajar.

—

English: I once took a train to a ski resort. It was a very comfortable ride.

Spanish: Una vez tomé un tren para ir a un resort de esquiar. Fue un viaje muy cómodo.

—

English: There is a baby crying next to me on the plane.

Spanish: Hay un bebe llorando a mi lado en el avión.

—

English: Have a safe flight! Let me know when you land.

Spanish: ¡Espero tengas un vuelo seguro! Avísame al aterrizar.

—

English: Remember to take your passport with you, otherwise you won't be able to fly.

Spanish: Recuerda llevar tu pasaporte contigo, de lo contrario no podrás volar.

—

English: Oh no! I lost my passport!

Spanish: ¡Oh no! He perdido mi pasaporte!

—

English: Hurry up or we will miss our flight!

Spanish: ¡Rápido o vamos a perder el vuelo!

—

English: The flight was cancelled due to bad weather. They will be flying tomorrow morning.

Spanish: El vuelo fue cancelado por mal clima Viajarán mañana en la mañana.

—

English: Laura and Jose are taking a honeymoon trip to Las Bahamas. They have been waiting for this moment for months.

Spanish: Laura y José tendrán su luna de miel en Las Bahamas. Llevan meses esperando este momento.

—

English: Maria visits her mother every month. She takes a train to her hometown and arrives in less than one hour.

Spanish: Maria visita a su madre cada mes. Ella toma un tren a su pueblo que llega en menos de una hora.

—

English: We were late to the airport and missed our flight.

Spanish: Llegamos tarde al aeropuerto y perdimos nuestro vuelo.

—

English: The line at the airport was very long, Pedro was afraid he would miss his flight.

Spanish: La fila en el aeropuerto estaba muy larga. Pedro temía perder su vuelo.

—

English: Leo took a surprise trip to visit his girlfriend.

Spanish: Leo tomó un viaje sorpresa para visitar a su novia.

—

English: Traveling takes you out of your comfort zone.

Spanish: Viajar te saca de tu zona de comfort.

—

English: The world is beautiful, that is enough reason to travel.

Spanish: El mundo es bello, esa es razón suficiente para viajar.

—

English: The first time I got on a plane I felt very scared.

Spanish: La primera vez que me subí a un avión me sentí muy asustado.

—

English: I would love to travel for a living.

Spanish: Me encantaría viajar como trabajo.

—

English: We must convert our currencies before we visit a new country.

Spanish: Necesitamos cambiar nuestro dinero antes de visitar un nuevo país.

—

English: Clark lost his luggage when he landed. He had to buy new clothes for the trip.

Spanish: Clark perdió su equipaje cuando aterrizó. Tuvo que comprar ropa nueva para el viaje.

—

English: There are many restaurants and stores in the airport we can visit.

Spanish: Hay muchos restaurantes y tiendas en el aeropuerto que podemos visitar.

—

English: Remember to take your own headphones when you travel.

Spanish: Recuerda llevar tus auriculares cuando viajas.

—

English: Manuel has been flying for so long he got a free upgrade to first-class.

Spanish: Manuel ha viajado por tanto tiempo que lo promovieron a primera clase totalmente gratis.

—

English: I was surprised we landed so quickly.

Spanish: Me sorprendió que aterrizáramos tan rápido.

—

English: Do you want to rent a car and take a trip somewhere?

Spanish: ¿Te gustaría alquilar un coche e irnos de viaje a algún sitio?

—

English: Sure! What do you have in mind? Perhaps a good beach would be fun.

Spanish: ¡Claro! ¿Qué tienes en mente? A lo mejor una buena playa sería divertido.

—

English: Spring Break is a popular week to travel.

Spanish: La semana de pascua es muy popular para viajar.

—

English: We are going on a ski trip this Christmas. This will be our first time seeing snow.

Spanish: Nos vamos a un paseo de ski en Navidad. Esta será nuestra primera vez viendo la nieve.

—

English: Charging your phone before you travel is always a good idea.

Spanish: Siempre es buena idea cargar tu móvil antes de viajar.

—

English: We arrived in no time!

Spanish: ¡Llegamos de una vez!

—

English: Luis read a magazine while Pedro watched a movie next to him.

Spanish: Luis leía una revista mientras Pedro veía una película a su lado.

—

English: This is the third time I'm boarding a plane this month.

Spanish: Esta es la tercera vez en el mes que abordo un avión.

—

English: Pedro is always home alone. Her mother travels for a living.

Spanish: Pedro siempre está solo en casa. Su madre viaja como trabajo.

—

English: The pilot announced that the flight would be delayed by 10 minutes.

Spanish: El piloto anunció que el vuelo se iba a retrasar por diez minutos.

—

English: Jason knew he landed when every passenger started to clap.

Spanish: Jason supo que aterrizó cuando los pasajeros empezaron a aplaudir.

—

English: Before departing, the airline will play a video going over the safety instructions.

Spanish: Antes de despegar, la aerolínea mostrará un video repasando las instrucciones de seguridad.

—

English: My dream job would be an airplane pilot or ship captain.

Spanish: El trabajo de mi sueños sería piloto de avión o capitán de barco.

—

English: The ship left the harbor as it prepared to leave.

Spanish: El barco zarpó del muelle mientras se preparaba para irse.

—

English: Is Michael coming with us or is he taking the next flight.

Spanish: ¿Michael viene con nosotros o estará tomando el próximo vuelo?

—

English: We need to take two cabs to the airport because the luggage won't fit.

Spanish: Necesitamos tomar dos taxis para el aeropuerto porque nuestro equipaje no cabe en uno.

—

English: Don't worry; we will make it on time.

Spanish: No te preocupes, llegaremos a tiempo.

—

English: This was one of the best vacations ever! We should definitely do it again.

Spanish: Esta ha sido una de las mejores vacaciones que he tenido. Definitivamente tenemos que repetirla.

—

English: I can't believe we are going back home.

Spanish: No puedo creer que tengamos que regresar a casa.

—

English: All good things come to an end.

Spanish: Todas las cosas buenas tienen su final.

—

STORY-TIME Chapter 2: We Missed The Flight (English)

Manuel and his brother Jose were planning a trip to Miami for summer. They had a detailed itinerary of activities they would do and places they planned on visiting. However, on the day of the flight, Manuel forgot to set his alarm clock. As a result, he woke up 2 hours later than anticipated.

Manuel: Oh no! I can't believe I'm waking up this late. Jose, please wake up!

Jose: Give me five more minutes.

Manuel: We don't have five more minutes!

Jose: What time is it?

Manuel: We are two hours late!

Manuel and Jose got up, took a bath, and called a taxi to pick them up. The taxi also took longer than anticipated and they lost another hour. After finally arriving at the airport, Manuel and Jose tried to check in but they were told the flight was already long gone.

Manuel: This is the worst day of my life.

Customer Service Agent: Don't worry, we will book you another flight for tomorrow. Make sure to arrive early next time.

Manuel: Will do! Thank you!

The next day, Manuel and Jose arrived at the airport 3 hours earlier than anticipated. They learned their lesson and had an incredible time in Miami.

STORY-TIME Chapter 1: Perdimos El Vuelo (Español)

Manuel y su hermano José estaban planeando un viaje a Miami en verano. Tenían un itinerario detallado de actividades que iban a realizar y lugares que visitarían. Sin embargo, el día del vuelo Manuel olvidó programar su alarma despertadora. Como resultado, se despertó dos horas más tarde de lo anticipado.

Manuel: ¡Oh no! ¡No puedo creer que me estoy despertando tan tarde! José ¡por favor despierta!

José: Dame cinco minutos más.

Manuel: ¡No tenemos cinco minutos!

José: ¿Qué hora es?

Manuel: ¡Estamos dos horas tarde!

Manuel y José se levantaron, ducharon, y llamaron a un taxi para que los llevara al aeropuerto. El taxi también tardó más de lo anticipado y perdieron otra hora. Cuando finalmente llegaron al aeropuerto,

Manuel y José intentaron registrarse para el vuelo pero le comunicaron que este ya había despegado.

Manuel: Este es el peor día de mi vida.

Agente de Servicio al Cliente: No te preocupes, te estamos registrando para el vuelo de mañana. Procura llegar temprano la próxima vez.

Manuel: ¡Eso haré! Gracias

El día siguiente, Manuel y José llegaron al aeropuerto tres horas antes de lo anticipado. Aprendieron la lección y tuvieron unas vacaciones increíbles en Miami.

CHAPTER TWO TEST.

1 What does "aeropuerto" mean?
a) Airport
b) Airline
c) Airplane
d) None of the above

2 What does "tren" mean?
a) Train
b) Tray
c) Sister
d) Three

3 How do you say "travel" in Spanish?
a) Crucero
b) Avión

c)   Viajar
d)   Volar

4 How do invite someone to go on a trip with you?
a)   A qué hora es nuestro vuelo?
b)   Estamos a tiempo?
c)   Te gustaría viajar conmigo?
d)   De dónde eres?

5 What word means boat.
a)   Barco
b)   Tren
c)   Viajar
d)   Avión

_____

_____

Answers: 1) a, 2) a, 3) c, 4) c, 5) a.

_____

_____

Part Three: Food and Restaurants

Way to go! You are now two chapters in and ready to take on the third chapter of your Spanish learning experience. This chapter will focus on food and restaurants. At the end, you'll be able to order your favorite dishes in Spanish. Remember, practice as much as you can before you try our test. Feel free to go over if you need to review certain words of phrases. With that said, let's get started with Chapter 3.

English: I want to go to a restaurant tonight!

Spanish: ¡Quiero ir a un restaurante esta noche!

—

English: Are you in the mood for some sushi?

Spanish: ¿Estas en humor para sushi?

—

English: I'm on a diet, I can only eat food low in carbs.

Spanish: Estoy a dieta, solo puedo comer alimentos bajo en carbohidratos.

English: I heard there is a new restaurant in town. Their speciality is seafood.

Spanish: Escuche que hay un nuevo restaurante en el pueblo. Su especialidad es la comida del mar.

—

English: My favorite food is Italian. I love spaghettis and meatballs more than anything.

Spanish: Mi comida favorita es la Italiana. Me encantan los espaguetis con albóndigas más que nada.

—

English: Manuel took Laura on a date to a fancy restaurant.

Spanish: Manuel llevó a Laura a una cita en un restaurante muy lujoso.

—

English: What would you like to order?

Spanish: ¿Qué te interesa ordenar?

—

English: Can I get a glass of water with ice?

Spanish: ¿Me puede traer un vaso de agua con hielo?

—

English: As an entree, I recommend bread with olive oil.

Spanish: Como entrada, te puedo recomendar pan con aceite de oliva.

—

English: I prefer fast food restaurants over traditional ones.

Spanish: Prefiero los restaurantes de comida rápida sobre los tradicionales.

—

English: Fast food restaurants are very unhealthy.

Spanish: Los restaurantes de comida rápida son muy poco saludables.

—

English: I will order steak, but make sure it is well done.

Spanish: Quiero ordenar carne, pero asegúrate que este en término medio.

—

English: He ordered a hamburger with fries, but they forgot to add ketchup.

Spanish: El ordenó una hamburguesa con papas fritas, pero olvidaron la salsa de tomate.

—

English: I would go with you to eat, but I have no money.

Spanish: Iría contigo a comer, pero no tengo dinero.

—

English: I think they accept credit cards.

Spanish: Creo que aceptan tarjetas de crédito.

—

English: Don't worry, the food is on me!

Spanish: No te preocupes ¡yo invito!

—

English: He ordered a chicken breast for lunch, but it was very bland.

Spanish: Él ordenó una pechuga de pollo para almorzar, pero estaba muy blanda.

—

English: Welcome to the restaurant, table for how many?

Spanish: Bienvenidos al restaurante ¿mesa para cuantos?

—

English: Before we go to the restaurant we must first make a reservation.

Spanish: Antes de ir al restaurante debemos hacer una reservación.

—

English: Call the restaurant to make a reservation, I heard it's always full.

Spanish: Llama al restaurante para hacer una reserva. Escuche que siempre están llenos.

—

English: There is a famous chef in town, I heard he was going to cook in the city's restaurant.

Spanish: Hay un famoso cocinero en el pueblo. Escuche que iba a cocinar en el restaurante de la ciudad.

—

English: We can now use our phones to order food and have it delivered straight home.

Spanish: Ahora podemos usar nuestros teléfonos móviles para ordenar comida y que la entreguen directo en casa.

—

English: The delivery driver took forever and the food arrived cold as ice.

Spanish: El repartidor tardó demasiado y la comida llegó fría como el hielo.

—

English: Can I please have a steak with a glass of wine?

Spanish: ¿Me puede traer una carne con una copa de vino?

—

English: Breakfast is my favorite time of the day.

Spanish: El desayuno es mi tiempo favorito del día.

—

English: I love eggs and ham for breakfast.

Spanish: Yo amo huevos y jamón para desayuno.

—

English: Excuse me, waiter! Can I have the menu, please?

Spanish: ¡Disculpa, camarero! ¿Me puede traer el menú, por favor?

—

English: Just a moment, how many menus would you want?

Spanish: Solo un momento ¿cuántos menús vas a querer?

—

English: Let me know once you've made up your mind and are ready to order.

Spanish: Me avisas cuando se hayan decidido y estén listos para ordenar.

—

English: Just a moment, we will be ready in a couple of minutes.

Spanish: Solo un momento, estaremos listos en varios minutos.

—

English: Do you have any recommendations for us? What is the best plate on the menu?

Spanish: ¿Tienes alguna recomendación para nosotros? ¿Cuál es el mejor plato en el menú?

—

English: I recommend the penne a la vodka with mashed potatoes and a good bottle of wine.

Spanish: Te recomiendo el penne a la vodka con puré de papas y una buena botella de vino.

—

English: What would you like to drink?

Spanish: ¿Que vas a querer para beber?

—

English: I want a glass of water. She would like a coke, and he would like to order a coke.

Spanish: Yo quiero una copa de agua. Ella quiere una coca-cola, y él otra también.

—

English: Do you have a menu for desserts?

Spanish: ¿Tiene un menú para postres?

—

English: I'm in the mood for something sweet, perhaps some ice-cream.

Spanish: Tengo ganas de algo dulce, a lo mejor helado.

—

English: My favorite dessert is cheesecake.

Spanish: Mi postre favorito es el cheesecake.

—

English: The restaurant is packed, I guess we will have to cook at home.

Spanish: El restaurante está lleno, tendremos que cocinar en casa.

—

English: Here is your check, sir. Would you like to pay in cash or credit card?

Spanish: Aquí esta su cuenta, señor. ¿Le gustaría pagar en efectivo o con tarjeta de crédito?

—

English: Don't forget to tip your waiter if he did a good job.

Spanish: No te olvides de dejar propina a tu camarero si hizo un buen trabajo.

—

English: Most restaurants have a bar for people to drink and have fun.

Spanish: La mayoría de los restaurantes tienen un bar para que las personas beban y se diviertan.

—

English: I made a reservation for four at eight o clock.

Spanish: Hice una reservación para cuatro personas a las ocho.

—

English: I'm a good cook, or at least they tell me I am.

Spanish: Soy un buen cocinero, o al menos me dicen que lo soy.

—

English: I'm learning how to cook. As of now, I only know the basics.

Spanish: Estoy aprendiendo a cocinar. Por el momento, solo conozco lo básico.

—

English: The chef must first defrost the meat before cooking it.

Spanish: El cocinero debe primero descongelar la carne antes de cocinarla.

—

English: I want scrambled eggs for breakfast.

Spanish: Quiero huevos revueltos para desayuno.

—

English: I'm on a seafood diet. I see food and I eat it.

Spanish: Estoy en una dieta de comida marina. Veo comida y me la como.

—

English: Daniela is a vegetarian. That means she does not eat meat.

Spanish: Daniela es vegetariana. Eso significa que no come carne.

—

English: On Sundays my family always cooks meat on the barbecue.

Spanish: Mi familia siempre cocina carne en la barbacoa los domingos.

—

English: If you're on a diet, you should be eating chicken and rice.

Spanish: Si estas a dieta, deberías comer pollo y arroz.

—

English: Make sure you have a balanced diet and eat vegetables as well.

Spanish: Asegúrate de tener una dieta balanceada y comer vegetales también.

—

English: Life is too short to eat bad food.

Spanish: La vida es muy corta para comer comida mala.

—

English: Girls love a man who can cook.

Spanish: A las chicas les gustan los hombres que saben cocinar.

—

English: Luisa showed me a picture of a plate and it made me very hungry.

Spanish: Luisa me enseño una foto de un plato y me dio mucha hambre.

—

English: The food was delicious!

Spanish: La comida estaba deliciosa!

—

English: Wow that was amazing! I didn't know you knew how to cook.

Spanish: ¡Guao, eso estaba asombroso! No tenía idea qué sabias cocinar.

—

English: That lobster looks mouth-watering!

Spanish: Esa langosta esta para babear.

—

English: Excuse me, Maria. Could you please pass me the salt?

Spanish: Disculpa, Maria. Me puedes pasar la sal?

—

English: I'm trying to lose some weight so I won't be eating that much.

Spanish: Estoy intentando perder peso entonces no estaré comiendo mucho.

—

English: A home-cooked meal is always better than a fancy dish at a restaurant.

Spanish: Una comida casera siempre es mejor que un plato lujoso en un restaurante.

—

English: I want to eat some fried chicken!

Spanish: ¡Yo quiero comer pollo frito!

—

English: I prefer to have a grilled chicken breast, it is a healthier option.

Spanish: Prefiero una pechuga de pollo a la parrilla, es una opción más saludable.

—

English: An apple a day will keep the doctors away.

Spanish: Una manzana al día mantiene a los doctores lejos.

—

English: I love bacon, even more if you add some eggs to it.

Spanish: Yo amo la tocineta, aún más si le agregas huevos.

—

English: When life gives you lemons you need to make lemonade.

Spanish: Cuando la vida te da limones haz limonada.

—

English: Restaurants with live music are like magic.

Spanish: Los restaurantes con música en vivo son como magia.

—

English: The food tastes as sweet as honey.

Spanish: La comida sabe tan dulce como la miel.

—

English: Do you have food delivery services?

Spanish: ¿Tienes servicio de comida a domicilio?

—

English: Do you have any food allergies?

Spanish: ¿Tienes alguna alergia de comida?

—

English: I'm allergic to peanuts, so I can't eat peanut butter.

Spanish: Soy alérgico a las nueces, no puedo comer mantequilla de maní.

—

English: I always eat a ham and cheese sandwich for breakfast.

Spanish: Yo siempre me como un sándwich de jamón y queso para el desayuno.

—

English: I prefer a peanut butter and jelly sandwich.

Spanish: Yo prefiero un sándwich de mantequilla de maní y jalea.

—

English: Nothing like hot bread fresh out of the oven.

Spanish: Nada como pan caliente fresco fuera del horno.

—

English: You should store the food on the fridge or else it will rot.

Spanish: Deberías guardas la comida en el refrigerador o se va a pudrir.

—

English: Manuel's mom bought fruits and vegetables. She wants him to eat healthy.

Spanish: La madre de Manuel compró frutas y vegetales. Ella quiere que el coma saludable.

—

English: Apples and oranges are two fruits I don't like.

Spanish: Las manzanas y las naranjas son dos frutas que no me gustan.

—

English: I heard mangoes are really sweet but I have never tried them.

Spanish: Yo escuché que los mangos son muy dulces pero nunca los he probado.

—

English: Forget about fruits, I will always choose meat over everything.

Spanish: Olvídate de las frutas, yo siempre voy a escoger carne sobre todo.

—

English: The food tasted so good that he ordered another plate just like it.

Spanish: La comida estuvo tan buena que el ordenó otro plato igual.

—

English: Stunning experience, we will definitely return to this restaurant.

Spanish: Experiencia impactante, nosotros vamos a volver a este restaurante definitivamente.

—

STORY-TIME Chapter 3: A Special Surprise (English)

Luisa and her friends were planning to have a very special Friday night. She made reservations to one of the most famous restaurants in the city. Rumor said that one popular Michelin chef was going to be cooking there that night. Luisa was very excited and, as a food lover herself, Friday couldn't come quick enough.

The big day came and Luisa dressed elegantly, called a taxi, and picked up her friends to take them to the famous restaurant. Once there, they all noticed the restaurant was packed with people. Thank God, Luisa made a reservation.

Waiter: Welcome to the restaurant, do you have a reservation?

Luisa: Hello! Yes we have, my name is Luisa. I called two days ago.

Waiter: Hmm, Luisa. We don't see any Luisa here.

Luisa: That's weird, I'm pretty sure they confirmed the reservation.

Waiter: Sorry, but we can't let you in without one. The tables are all full.

Luisa: What!

Luisa was getting angry, but she kept her cool. She had been waiting for this day forever, and nothing was taking that from her. Luisa, focused on getting her table, asked to speak with the manager. But, something even better happened. The famous chef overheard the conversation and surprised her with something special.

Chef: Hello Luisa, I couldn't help overhearing your conversation and I have a solution.

Luisa: Oh my god! You are the famous chef!

Chef: Yes I am. How would you like to sit at our table?

Luisa: Really?

Chef: Absolutely, and don't worry about the check, everything is on me. Get ready to eat some good food.

Luisa couldn't believe it. Everything turned out for the better. The chef served them caviar for entree, delicious pasta for the main course and, to top it all off, a vanilla ice cream for dessert. They had an amazing time together and Luisa even took a picture with the famous chef. A night for the books.

STORY-TIME Chapter 3: Una Sorpresa Especial (Español)

Luis y sus amigas estaban planeando tener un viernes nocturno muy especial. Ella hizo reservaciones para uno de los restaurantes más famosos de la ciudad. Los rumores apuntaban a que un cocinero muy popular con estrellas Michelin iba a estar cocinando esa noche. Luisa estaba muy emocionada y, como amante de la comida, no podía esperar al viernes.

El gran día llegó y Luisa se vistió muy elegante, llamó a un taxi, y buscó a sus amigas para luego ir al famoso restaurante. Una vez allí, todas se dieron cuenta que el restaurante estaba lleno de personas. Gracias a Dios Luisa hizo una reservación.

Camarero: Bienvenidas al restaurante, tienen una reservación?

Luisa: ¡Hola! Si tenemos, mi nombre es Luisa. Llame hace dos días.

Camarero: Hmm, Luisa. No vemos a ninguna Luisa aquí.

Luisa: Qué raro, estoy muy segura que confirmaron mi reservación.

Camarero: Disculpa, pero no te podemos dar entrada sin una. Las mesas están todas ocupadas.

Luisa: ¡Que!

Luisa se estaba enojando, pero mantuvo la cordura. Ella tenía mucho tiempo esperando este día, y nada ni nadie se lo iba a quitar. Luisa, enfocada en conseguir su mesa, preguntó por el gerente. Sin embargo, algo mejor pasó. El famoso cocinero escuchó la conversación y la sorprendió con algo muy especial.

Cocinero: Hola Luisa, no pude evitar escuchar tu conversación y tengo una solución.

Luisa: ¡Oh Dios mío! ¿Tú eres el cocinero famoso?

Cocinero: Así es. Te gustaría sentarte en nuestra mesa?

Luisa: En serio?

Cocinero: Claro que si, y no te preocupes por la cuenta, yo pago todo. Prepárate para comer buena comida.

Luisa no lo podía creer. Todo salió mejor que lo planeado. El cocinero les sirvió caviar de entrada, una deliciosa pasta para el plato fuerte y, para concluir, un helado de vainilla para el postre. Tuvieron un tiempo increíble y Luisa hasta se tiró una foto con el famoso cocinero. Una noche para la historia.

CHAPTER THREE TEST.

1 In the story above, why was Luisa angry?
a)   She was feeling bad.
b)   She was very hungry.

c) Her name was not on the reservation.
d) None of the above

2 What does "chef" mean?
a) Cocinero
b) Camarero
c) Comida
d) Restaurante

3 How do you say "check" in Spanish?
a) Restaurante
b) Carne
c) Postre
d) Cuenta

4 What is a main dish in Spanish?
a) Plato fuerte o plato principal.
b) Postre
c) Entrada
d) Cocinero

5 What word means dessert in Spanish.
a) Postre
b) Comida
c) Pasta
d) Reservación

_____

_____

Answers: 1) c, 2) a, 3) d, 4) a, 5) a.

_____

_____

Part Four: Animals

Look at you! You have sailed through three chapters of this Spanish learning course. You can now introduce yourself to new people, order at your favorite restaurants, and more. In this chapter, we will introduce you to the animal kingdom and all the wonders it has to offer. You will learn the names of all your favorite animals and interesting phrases you can use to practice. Remember, practice makes perfect, so be sure to master this chapter before skipping ahead to the next. Off we go!

English: The dog is the world's most popular domestic pet.

Spanish: El perro es el animal doméstico más popular del mundo.

—

English: I love dogs, they are so cute!

Spanish: Amo los perros ¡son tan adorables!

—

English: I'm a cat person.

Spanish: Soy una persona de gatos.

—

English: Dogs are very smart, perhaps one of the smartest animals.

Spanish: Los perros son muy inteligentes, incluso son de los animales más inteligentes.

—

English: I want to adopt a puppy but my mother won't let me.

Spanish: Yo quiero adoptar un cachorro, pero mi madre no me permite.

—

English: Dogs are men's best friends.

Spanish: El perro es el mejor amigo del hombre.

—

English: The dog barked.

Spanish: El perro ladró.

—

English: Cats love to sleep. They can sleep all day.

Spanish: Los gatos aman dormir. Ellos pueden dormir todo el día.

—

English: What is your favorite animal?

Spanish: ¿Cuál es tu animal favorito?
—

English: My favorite animal is the monkey. I love how they resemble us.

Spanish: Mi animal favorito es el mono. Me gusta como se parecen a nosotros.

—

English: We should go visit the zoo. I heard they brought a tiger from India.

Spanish: Deberíamos visitar el zoológico. Escuché que trajeron a un tigre de India.

—

English: If we get a puppy you must promise me you will train him.

Spanish: Si compramos un cachorro me tienes que prometer que lo vas a entrenar.

—

English: Go take the dog out for a walk.

Spanish: Saca al perro a pasear.

—

English: My first pet was a turtle.

Spanish: Mi primera mascota fue una tortuga.

—

English: He ordered pork for lunch.

Spanish: El ordenó cerdo para el almuerzo.

—

English: Lions are the king of the jungle.

Spanish: El león es el rey de la selva.

—

English: I'm scared of reptiles.

Spanish: Le tengo miedo a los reptiles.

—

English: The crocodile lives in the swamp.

Spanish: El cocodrilo vive en el pantano.

—

English: The eagle is the symbol of liberty.

Spanish: El águila es el símbolo de libertad.

—

English: We went to the zoo to watch the penguins.

Spanish: Fuimos al zoológico a ver a los pingüinos.

—

English: We must protect all living creatures.

Spanish: Debemos proteger a todos los seres vivientes.

—

English: If we ever visit Africa, promise me you will take me to a safari.

Spanish: Si alguna vez vamos a visitar Africa, prométeme que me vas a llevar a un safari.

—

English: When I grow up I want to be a veterinarian.

Spanish: Cuando crezca quiero ser veterinario.

—

English: The pet industry is growing like no other.

Spanish: La industria de mascotas está creciendo como nunca.

—

English: Fishes make excellent house pets.

Spanish: Los peces son excelentes animales domésticos.

—

English: Horses look so majestic when they run.

Spanish: Los caballos lucen majestuosos cuando corren.

—

English: Remember, donkeys and horses might look alike but they are very different.

Spanish: Recuerda, los burros y caballos pueden lucir similares, pero son muy diferentes.

—

English: The ugly worm turned into a beautiful butterfly.

Spanish: La fea lombriz se convirtió en una hermosa mariposa.

—

English: There is a mouse in our house, so my mom bought a cat.

Spanish: Hay un ratón en la casa, así que mi madre trajo un gato.

—

English: The skunk left a terrible smell.

Spanish: El zorrillo dejó un olor terrible.

—

English: Some animals are carnivores, others are herbivores.

Spanish: Algunos animales son carnívoros, otros son herbívoros.

—

English: Carnivores eat meat, like the leopard.

Spanish: Los carnívoros comen carne, como el leopardo.

—

English: Herbivores eat grass and leaves, like giraffes.

Spanish: Los herbívoros comen grama y hojas, como las jirafas.

—

English: Omnivores can eat both meat and leaves as well. Those are very rare.

Spanish: Los omnívoros pueden comer tanto carne como hojas. Son muy escasos.

—

English: What came first the chicken or the egg?

Spanish: Que llegó primero ¿el huevo o la gallina?

—

English: Why did the chicken cross the road?

Spanish: ¿Por qué la gallina cruzo la calle?

—

English: An octopus has eight tentacles.

Spanish: El pulpo tiene ocho tentáculos.

—

English: Some snakes are venomous and others are not.

Spanish: Algunas serpientes son venenosas y otras no.

—

English: Frogs can also be venomous, some even lethal.

Spanish: Los sapos también pueden ser venenosos, incluso hasta letales.

—

English: Polar bears are similar to bears but they have white fur.

Spanish: Los osos polares son similares a los osos pero tienen el pelaje blanco.

—

English: Cheetahs are the world's fastest land animals.

Spanish: El cheetah es el animal terrestre más rápido del mundo.

—

English: Mosquitoes are annoying bugs.

Spanish: Los mosquitos son insectos desesperantes.

—

English: Some people like to keep tigers as pets. Sometimes it is best to leave Mother Nature alone.

Spanish: Algunas personas gustan tener tigres como mascotas. A veces es mejor dejar a la Madre Naturaleza tranquila.

—

English: Tonight we are cooking the fish we captured in the morning.

Spanish: Esta noche vamos a cocinar el pez que capturamos en la mañana.

—

English: Dolphins are the world's smartest animals.

Spanish: Los delfines son los animales mas inteligentes del mundo.

—

English: You can usually find bats hidden in dark caves.

Spanish: Puedes encontrar a los murciélagos escondidos en cuevas oscuras.

—

English: Ostriches can't fly but they sure can run fast.

Spanish: El avestruz no puede volar pero corren muy rápido.

—

English: He had a goat in his farm. It was very cute.

Spanish: Él tenía una cabra en su granja. Era adorable.

—

English: Some rabbits have dog complexes.

Spanish: Algunos conejos tienen complejo de perro.

—

English: Ducks like to swim in ponds.

Spanish: A los patos le gusta nadar en lagos.

—

English: Have you even seen a Komodo dragon?

Spanish: Alguna vez has visto a un dragón de Komodo?

—

English: I haven't, but one time I saw a grizzly bear.

Spanish: No, pero una vez vi a un oso.

—

English: Wild animals are driven by instinct.

Spanish: Los animales salvajes se mueven por instinto.

—

English: There are very few domestic animals compared to the amount of animals in the world.

Spanish: Hay muy pocos animales domésticos comparado a la cantidad de animales en el mundo.

—

English: Some animals carry deadly diseases with them.

Spanish: Algunos animales portan enfermedades letales.

—

English: You should stay away from those types of animals.

Spanish: Tienes que mantenerte alejado de esos tipos de animales.

—

English: The dog bit me.

Spanish: El perro me mordió.

—

English: The cat scratched me when it got angry.

Spanish: El gato rasga cuando se enoja.

—

English: Manuel surprised his little brother with a puppy for his birthday.

Spanish: Manuel sorprendió su hermano menor con un cachorro para su cumpleaños.

—

English: Animals have a six sense when it comes to predicting natural disasters.

Spanish: Los animales tienen un sexto sentido para predecir desastres naturales.

—

English: We should all respect Mother Nature.

Spanish: Todos debemos respetar a la Madre Naturaleza.

—

English: The forest is home to many exciting animals.

Spanish: La selva es el hogar de muchos animales interesantes.

—

English: Lions live in the savannah.

Spanish: Los leones viven en la sabana.

—

English: Gorillas are very powerful.

Spanish: Los gorilas son muy poderosos.

—

English: Squirrels are funny animals, they also eat nuts.

Spanish: Las ardillas son animales chistosos, también comen nueces.

—

English: The big blue whale is a majestic creature.

Spanish: La gran ballena azul es una criatura majestuosa.

—

English: The pelican dived into the ocean.

Spanish: El pelicano se sumergió al océano.

—

English: Lizards can usually be found climbing trees.

Spanish: Los lagartos usualmente pueden ser encontrados escalando arboles.

—

English: They say a cockroach can survive a nuclear attack.

Spanish: Dicen que una cucaracha puede sobrevivir un ataque nuclear.

—

English: Pablo's sister is afraid of spiders.

Spanish: La hermana de Pablo le tiene miedo a las arañas.

—

English: Cows are my favorite farm animal.

Spanish: Las vacas son mi animal de granja favorito.

—

English: Elephants are very playful, but they are scared of mice.

Spanish: Los elefantes son muy juguetones, pero le tienen miedo a los ratones.

—

English: Kangaroos can only be found in Australia.

Spanish: Los canguros solo pueden ser encontrados en Australia.

—

English: Bears hibernate for a long time.

Spanish: Los osos hibernan por mucho tiempo.

—

English: Giraffes have a very long neck. They use it to reach fruits in tall places.

Spanish: Las jirafas tienen un cuello largo. Lo usan para alcanzar las frutas en altos lugares.

—

English: Birds fly, fish swim, and tigers run.

Spanish: Las aves vuelan, los peces nadas, y los tigres corren.

—

English: The lifeguard saw a big white shark approaching the shore.

Spanish: El salvavidas vio a un tiburón blanco acercándose a la costa.

—

English: My grandfather took me fishing. We caught a big marlin.

Spanish: Mi abuela me llevo de pesca. Capturamos a un gran marlín.

—

English: The ocean is big and mysterious. Just imagine all the creatures that live in it.

Spanish: El océano es grande y misterioso. Solo imaginate todas las criaturas que viven en el.

—

English: Whales might live in the ocean, but they are mammals.

Spanish: Las ballenas pueden vivir en el océano, pero siguen siendo mamíferos.

—

STORY-TIME Chapter 4: MS. Jane (English)

To say Ms. Jane likes animals would be an understatement. Since a young age she has been fascinated with all sorts of exotic animals from all around the world and because she is fabulously rich, she bought all her favorite animals and keeps them in her large mansion.

Kim: Honey! Can I ask you a couple of questions? It's for Tommy's homework.

Jane: Sure.

Kim: What color is your parrot of Asia?

Jane: It's white, green and pink.

Kim: Right. What color is your Arabian camel?

Jane: it's brown.

Kim: OK. What color is your Persian cat?

Jane: My adorable and beautiful Persian cat is white.

Kim: Sure. What color is your American spider?

Jane: Black and gray! And I don't want to answer any more questions Kim

Kim: Please Aunt Jane! Did I already tell you that your red hair looks fabulous on you?

Jane: What? It's midnight honey! I have to work tomorrow. Good night.

STORY-TIME Capítulo 4: SRA. Jane (Español)

Decir que a la Sra. Jane le gustan los animales sería quedarse corto. Desde pequeña ha estado fascinada con todo tipo de animales exóticos de todo el mundo y, como es fabulosamente rica, compró todos sus animales favoritos y los guarda en su gran mansión.

Kim: ¡Cariño! ¿Puedo hacerte un par de preguntas? Es para la tarea de Tommy.

Jane: Claro.

Kim: ¿De qué color es tu loro de Asia?

Jane: Es blanco, verde y rosado.

Kim: Correcto. ¿De qué color es tu camello árabe?

Jane: es marrón.

Kim: Está bien. ¿De qué color es tu gato persa?

Jane: Mi adorable y hermoso gato persa es blanco.

Kim: Claro. ¿De qué color es tu araña americana?

Jane: ¡Negra y gris! Y no quiero responder más preguntas, Kim.

Kim: ¡Por favor tía Jane! ¿Ya te dije que tu cabello rojo te queda fabuloso?

Jane: ¿Qué? ¡Es medianoche, cariño! Tengo que trabajar mañana. Buenas noches.

—

CHAPTER FOUR TEST.

1 What color is the sky?
A Azul
B Gris
C Amarillo
D Morado

2 What color is the sun?
A Rojo
B Amarillo
C Marrón
D Blanco

3 What color are the clouds?
A Rojo
B Blanco
C Negro
D Verde

4 What color is the koala?
A Gris
B Rosa
C Naranja
D Violeta

5 What word means 'Rosado'
A Blue
B Green
C Silver
D Pink

Answers: 1) a, 2) b, 3) b, 4) a, 5) d.

Part Five: Friendship and Conversation

Welcome to chapter five, a whole new world awaits you. After finishing this chapter, you will learn how to make new friends and keep conversations going. You will also know how to communicate drama and understand others when they speak about romantic things. Lets go!

English: Hello Andrew! Do you need some company?

Spanish: ¡Hola Andrew! ¿Necesitas compañía?

—

English: Hi Sarah! Yeah, of course

Spanish: ¡Hola Sara! Sí, por supuesto

—

English: What about your day? I was playing piano

Spanish: ¿Qué tal tu día? Yo estaba tocando el piano

—

English: I was watering my plants, thanks for asking

Spanish: Estaba regando mis plantas, gracias por preguntar

—

English: My mother is a very talented gardener

Spanish: Mi madre es una jardinera talentosa

—

English: Oh cool! That's amazing

Spanish: ¡Oh genial!

—

English: Do you want to come to my house someday?

Spanish: ¿Quieres venir a mi casa algún día?

—

English: That's a deal!

Spanish: ¡Es un trato!

—

English: My mother will love you! You are so interesting

Spanish: ¡Mi madre te amará! Eres muy interesante

—

English: ¿What about him? I think he is very selfish

Spanish: ¿Por qué me preguntas sobre él? Creo que es un egoísta.

—

English: Really? Why?

Spanish: ¿De verdad? ¿Por qué?

—

English: He only thinks of himself. That sucks!

Spanish: Él solo piensa en sí mismo. ¡Eso apesta!

—

English: Well, I need to tell you something

Spanish: Bueno, necesito contarte algo

—

English: You are scaring me. What happened?

Spanish: Me estás asustando. ¿Qué sucedió?

English: Peter is my new boyfriend and I didn't know that you didn't like him

Spanish: Peter es mi nuevo novio y yo no sabía que él no te gustaba.

—

English: C'mon Sarah! He is very stupid, egocentric and…

Spanish: ¡Vamos Sarah! Él es muy estúpido, egocéntrico y…

—

English: And what? Tell me!

Spanish: ¿Y qué? ¡Dímelo!

—

English: Sorry Sarah but this is very difficult to say

Spanish: Lo siento Sarah pero esto es muy difícil de decir

—

English: Please, tell me. You are my friend

Spanish: Por favor dímelo, tú eres mi amigo

—

English: He is cheating on you

Spanish: Él está engañándote

—

English: How is it possible? I can't believe you sorry Andrew

Spanish: ¿Cómo es posible? No puedo creerte, lo siento Andrew

—

English: Are you crazy Sarah? You have to believe me!

Spanish: ¿Estás loca Sarah? ¡Tienes que creerme!

—

English: What about our friendship?

Spanish: ¿Y qué hay sobre nuestra Amistad?

—

English: I think you are jealous, probably you love me

Spanish: Creo que estás celoso, probablemente me amas

—

English: I don't love you! Well, I love you but as a friend

Spanish: ¡No te amo! Bueno, te amo pero como a un amigo

—

English: I don't need your friendship Andrew

Spanish: Ya no necesito tu amistad Andrew

—

English: What are you talking about? ¿What did I do?

Spanish: ¿De qué estás hablando? ¿Qué hice?

—

English: You have nerve!

Spanish: ¡Eres un caradura!

—

English: Well, if you don't mind, I'll stay with you. You don't know what you are saying

Spanish: Bueno, si no te molesta, me quedaré a tu lado. No sabes lo que dices

—

English: I am not a baby Andrew and you are not my father

Spanish: No soy un bebé Andrew y tampoco eres mi padre

—

English: Thanks God for that! I know what I am, I am your friend

Spanish: ¡Gracias a Dios por eso! Sé lo que soy, soy tu amigo

—

English: Now Peter is all I need, you are jealous because you don't have a girlfriend

Spanish: Ahora Peter es todo lo que necesito, estás celoso porque no tienes novia

—

English: Sarah I don´t know you. You are very different now

Spanish: Sarah ya no te conozco. Eres tan diferente ahora

—

English: Sorry…I don't know what's happening to me

Spanish: Lo siento…no sé qué me está sucediendo

—

English: What's going on? You are very rude now

Spanish: ¿Qué te sucede? Eres tan grosera ahora

—

English: I need the attention of my parents. That's all.

Spanish: Necesito la atención de mis padres. Eso es todo

—

English: Oh my dear, I knew it! You are not that rude girl

Spanish: Oh cariño lo sabía, tú no eres esa chica grosera

—

English: They never talk with me!

Spanish: ¡Ellos nunca me hablan!

—

English: Sarah they are very busy.

Spanish: Sarah recuerda que ellos están muy ocupados.

—

English: I need more family time, I feel alone sometimes

Spanish: Necesito más tiempo en familia, me siento sola a veces

—

English: I am here for you. Don't forget that

Spanish: Estoy aquí para ti. No olvides eso

—

English: Thank you Andrew. You are a loyal friend

Spanish: Gracias Andrew. Eres un amigo muy fiel

—

English: And now? What about Peter?

Spanish: ¿Y ahora? ¿Qué harás con Peter?

—

English: Peter is history. Now I need to do something new

Spanish: Peter es historia. Ahora necesito hacer algo nuevo

—

English: Okay that's fine. Do you have something in mind?

Spanish: Genial, está bien. ¿Tienes algo en mente?

—

English: Maybe I need to red new books or water the plants with your mother

Spanish: Quizás necesito leer libros nuevos o regar plantas con tu madre

—

English: I think you need to go home and talk with your parents

Spanish: Creo que necesitas ir a casa y hablar con tus padres

—

English: I don't know, I think they don't love me. They just love Lizzie

Spanish: No lo sé, yo creo que no me quieren. Ellos solo quieren a Lizzie

—

English: C'mon Sarah. Lizzie is your little sister! And she is a cutie pie

Spanish: ¡Vamos Sarah! Lizzie es tu hermanita y es una dulzura

—

English: ¡Oh no! Now you love her more than me

Spanish: ¡Oh no! Ahora la amas a ella más que a mí

—

English: Sarah, you are overreacting. Calm down please

Spanish: Sarah, estás exagerando. Cálmate por favor

—

English: I have to admit that I feel a bit sad today

Spanish: Necesito admitir que me siento un poco triste hoy.

—

English: Why? You are surprising me

Spanish: ¿Por qué? Estás sorprendiéndome

—

English: Don't you remember? I told you

Spanish: ¿No lo recuerdas? Te lo dije

—

English: Because you didn't tell me anything.

Spanish: Porque tu no me lo dijiste.

—

English: Really? Well, I lost my gold fish

Spanish: ¿De verdad? Bueno, he perdido a mi pez dorado

—

English: But it's never too late to give you a big hug my friend

Spanish: Pero nunca es tarde para darte un gran abrazo amiga mía

—

English: Sarah! I have to tell you something. I had a party at my house yesterday and you didn't come.

Spanish: Sarah! Tengo que decirte algo. Tuve una fiesta ayer en casa y no viniste.

—

English: What? Last time I saw you was on the 20th and you hadn't mentioned it

Spanish: ¿Qué? La última vez que te vi fue el 20 y tú no lo mencionaste.

—

English: Did you spend the 21st with Peter?

Spanish: ¿Estuviste el 21 con Peter?

—

English: Yes I did

Spanish: Sí, así fue

—

English: He said that he had been inviting you to the party all day long.

Spanish: Él dijo que había estado recordándote la fiesta todo el día.

—

English: That's not true! In fact, I remember that before he left, I had asked him about you because he is your neighbor.

Spanish: ¡Eso no es cierto! De hecho, recuerdo que antes de irse, le había preguntado sobre ti porque eres su vecino

—

English: Well, he was at the party with his real girlfriend

Spanish: Bueno, él estaba en la fiesta con su verdadera novia

—

English: He is a bad boy!

Spanish: ¡Él es un chico malo!

—

English: Definitely you deserve more than that

Spanish: Definitivamente mereces más que eso

—

English: Yeah, I was thinking about Brad Pitt or James Franco

Spanish: Sí estaba pensando en Brad Pitt o James Franco

—

English: Oh Sarah you are very funny. I think they are not your style of men.

Spanish: Oh Sarah eres muy graciosa. Ellos no son tu tipo.

—

English: Really? What do you think about Chris Evans or Orlando Bloom?

Spanish: ¿En serio? ¿Y qué piensas sobre Chris Evans u Orlando Bloom?

—

English: I think that you are very creative

Spanish: Yo creo que eres muy creativa

—

English: Have you ever imagined being married to a celebrity?

Spanish: ¿Alguna vez has imaginado que estás casado con una celebridad?

—

English: Of course!

Spanish: Claro que sí!

—

English: I need a name! This is getting better

Spanish: ¡Necesito un nombre! Esto se está volviendo cada vez major

—

English: My crush is Sofia Vergara. I think she is so hot, I love her accent.

Spanish: Mi amor platónico es Sofía Vergara. Creo que es muy sexy y amo su acento.

—

English: Really? I think you need something more.

Spanish: ¿De verdad? Creo que necesitas algo más.

—

English: More than Sofia Vergara?

Spanish: ¿Más que Sofía Vergara?

—

English: I think that you and E.T are the best couple ever!

Spanish: ¡Creo que tú y E.T son la mejor pareja de todas!

—

English: Sarah you are impossible!

Spanish: ¡Sarah eres imposible!

—

STORY-TIME Chapter 5: Susan and Andrew (English)

Susan and Andrew are good friends. Since Susan moved to the city they stopped talking. Now Susan wants to move back again and Andrew is going to help her:

Susan: Hello my friend!

Andrew: Hi Susan you look so pretty!

Susan: Thank you! You look very handsome today.

Andrew: Thanks. So, how do you like your new flat?

Susan: It's great! But there are some weird tenants. I feel uncomfortable.

Andrew: You don't say!

Susan: I'm ok with that, it's only temporary though.

Andrew: Hey, you know what? I know what you should do.

Susan: What's that?

Andrew: My father owns an apartment in the center. You should check it out!

Susan: It sounds good! Let's go right now!

STORY-TIME Capítulo 5: Susan y Andrew (Español)

Susan y Andrew son buenos amigos. Desde que Susan se mudó a la ciudad dejaron de hablar. Ahora Susan quiere mudarse de nuevo y Andrew la ayudará:

Susan: ¡Hola mi amigo!

Andrew: ¡Hola Susan, te ves tan bonita!

Susan: ¡Gracias! Te ves muy guapo hoy.

Andrew: Gracias. Entonces, ¿qué te parece tu nuevo piso?

Susan: ¡Es genial! Pero hay algunos inquilinos extraños. Me siento incómoda.

Andrew: ¡No me digas!

Susan: Pero estoy tranquila con ello porque solo es temporal.

Andrew: Oye, ¿sabes qué? Sé lo que debes hacer.

Susan: ¿Qué debo hacer?

Andrew: Mi padre tiene un apartamento en el centro. ¡Deberías verlo!

Susan: ¡Suena bien! ¡Vamos ahora mismo!

———

CHAPTER FIVE TEST.

1. In the story above, why was Susan uncomfortable?

A Because of some weird plants

B Because of some weird tenants

C Because of some weird animals

D Because of some weird kids

2. What does "Friend" mcans?

A Amigo

B Tonto

C Padre

D Abuelo

3 How do you say "Flat" in Spanish?

A Hogar

B Jardin

C Terraza

D Piso

4 In the story above, where does Susan live?

A In the city

B In Germany

C In Austria

D In Russia

5 What word means "best friends"

A Novios

B Mejores amigos

C Prometidos

D Pareja

Answers: 1) b, 2) a, 3) d, 4) a, 5) b.

Part Six: News and Sports

Congratulations on breezing through chapter five, you are now halfway there. You've won half the battle but remember, learning a new language is all about practice and Spanish is no different. This chapter will cover everything related to news, sports, and television. You will learn the Spanish lingo used to discuss scores with your friends. Read, set, go!

English: This just in, a new female candidate has decided to run for mayor

Spanish: Acaba de postularse una candidata para alcaldesa

—

English: In our top story, we'll take a look at the ongoing criminal investigation

Spanish: En nuestra noticia del día, le daremos un vistazo a la investigación criminal del momento

—

English: Stay tuned for our exclusive interview with Donald Trump

Spanish: Manténgase allí para nuestra entrevista exclusiva con Donald Trump

—

English: This is Sharon, reporting live at the White House

Spanish: Soy Sharon, reportando en vivo desde La Casa Blanca

—

English: Let's hear from Julia, who's reporting live at the scene

Spanish: Ahora escuchemos a Julia que está reportando en vivo desde la escena

—

English: Now, back to you Kim

Spanish: Ahora, volvemos contigo Kim

—

English: Hello Mark do you want to play something?

Spanish: ¿Hola Mark quieres jugar algo?

—

English: Sorry Mike, I don't really like sports, I prefer watching TV.

Spanish: Lo siento Mike, no me gustan los deportes, prefiero ver televisión

—

English: Mark, sports are very fun. There is a huge variety of options for you to choose.

Spanish: Mark, los deportes son muy divertidos. Hay una enorme variedad de opciones para elegir

—

English: My favorite is football, but I also like basketball and ping pong

Spanish: Mi favorite es el fútbol pero también me gusta el básquet y el tenis de mesa

—

English: Have you seen the news today? I am shocked

Spanish: ¿Viste las noticias hoy? Estoy sorprendido

—

English: Did you know there was a blackout last night?

Spanish: ¿Supiste que anoche hubo un apagón?

—

English: Yes, I heard the lights were out all night

Spanish: Sí, escuché que hubo un apagón durante toda la noche

—

English: Hopefully we won't have any more blackouts

Spanish: Espero que no volvamos a tener más apagones en el futuro

—

English: We'd talk sports and stuff, and maybe have a beer

Spanish: Hablaríamos sobre deportes y eso, quizá nos bebamos una cerveza

—

English: A bunch of people went looting last night.

Spanish: Mucha gente fue anoche a saquear.

—

English: The news reported that four stores were broken into.

Spanish: Las noticias reportaron que cuatro tiendas fueron asaltadas.

—

English: Did the police find who did it? I didn't watch the news

Spanish: ¿La policía atrapó a quién lo hizo? No vi las noticias

—

English: There's no evidence of who did it.

Spanish: No hay evidencia de quién lo hizo.

—

English: Swimming is a very athletic sport

Spanish: Nadar es un deporte muy atlético

—

English: Playing sports is the healthiest way to have fun

Spanish: Hacer deportes es la forma más sana de divertirse

—

English: I love tennis and I adore the player Rafael Nadal

Spanish: El tenis me encanta y adoro al jugador Rafael Nadal

—

English: Jogging every day is good for the bones

Spanish: Trotar todos los días es beneficioso para los huesos

—

English: Climbing a mountain is very difficult but beautiful at the same time

Spanish: Escalar una montaña es muy difícil pero hermoso a la vez

—

English: Practicing gymnastics is a way to develop elasticity

Spanish: Practicar gimnasia es una forma de desarrollar la elasticidad

—

English: I don't want to run, I prefer to jump rope or dance salsa

Spanish: No quiero correr, prefiero saltar la cuerda o bailar salsa

—

English: My favorite sport would be to buy sports cars in Germany

Spanish: Mi deporte favorito sería comprar autos deportivos en Alemania

—

English: Swimming is the best way to take care of our lungs

Spanish: Nadar es la mejor forma de cuidar nuestros pulmones

—

English: What time is that soccer game on? I thought it started at noon.

Spanish: ¿A qué hora es ese partido de fútbol? Pensé que comenzaba al mediodía.

—

English: Soccer's not my favorite sport anyway. I much prefer basketball.

Spanish: El fútbol no es mi deporte favorito de todos modos. Prefiero el baloncesto.

—

English: What time is that soccer game on?

Spanish: ¿Cuándo comienza el partido de fútbol?

—

English: I like basketball a lot more than soccer

Spanish: Me gusta mucho más el baloncesto que el fútbol

—

English: Arnold lets play a basketball game!

Spanish: ¡Arnold juguemos un partido de baloncesto!

—

English: I am a big fan of rugby. Do you know that sport? It is very popular in New Zealand

Spanish: Soy un verdadero fanático del rugby. ¿Conoces ese deporte? Es muy famoso en Nueva Zelanda

—

English: Hockey on ice is my favourite sport. I really like that energy

Spanish: El hockey sobre hielo es mi deporte favorite. De verdad me encanta esa energía

—

English: We heard that detail on the late news.

Spanish: Nosotros escuchamos ese detalle en las noticias

—

English: I'm not sure how he's going to react to the news.

Spanish: No estoy seguro de cómo él va a reaccionar a las noticias

—

English: The good news is that tomorrow will be fine and sunny.

Spanish: La buena noticia es que mañana será un día genial y soleado

—

English: Do you have any news for me?

Spanish: ¿Tienes alguna noticia para mí?

—

English: Everyone is shocked by the news of the arrests.

Spanish: Todo el mundo está sorprendido por las noticias de los arrestos

—

English: Have you heard the news? We're going to get married.

Spanish: ¿Escuchaste las noticias? Nos vamos a casar

—

English: People living near an unused library received news that it is to be demolished.

Spanish: La gente que vive cerca de una biblioteca abandonada recibió la noticia de que será demolida

—

English: Friday's news was greeted with enthusiasm in South Africa

Spanish: Las noticias del viernes fueron acogidas con mucho entusiasmo en Sudáfrica

—

English: Sit down and tell me all your news.

Spanish: Siéntate y cuéntame todas tus noticias

—

English: What's the latest news on your university application?

Spanish: ¿Cuáles son las últimas noticias sobre la aplicación de tu universidad?

—

English: We are delighted at the news that your girlfriend is expecting a baby

Spanish: Estamos encantados con la noticia de que tu novia está embarazada

—

English: My favorita tennis player is Serena Williams

Spanish: Mi jugadora de tenis favorita es Serena Williams

—

English: ¿Is cricket a good sport? In my country it is not popular

Spanish: ¿El cricket es un buen deporte? En mi país no es popular

—

English: Please don't think that I am boring but my favourite sport is chess

Spanish: Por favor no creas que soy aburrido pero mi deporte favorito es el ajedrez

—

English: Winter sports are very popular in UK, not in America

Spanish: Los deportes de invierno son populares en Reino Unido, no en América

—

English: What do you do in your free time?

Spanish: ¿Qué te gusta hacer en tu tiempo libre?

—

English: Is it safe to swim here? I am afraid

Spanish: ¿Es seguro nadar aquí? Estoy asustado

—

English: Can one dive here without danger?

Spanish: ¿Se puede bucear aquí sin peligro?

—

English: Is there a dangerous undertow?

Spanish: ¿Hay una contracorriente peligrosa?

—

English: I like extreme sports, I can feel the adrenaline

Spanish: Me gustan los deportes extremos, puedo sentir la adrenalina

—

English: What time is low tide?

Spanish: ¿A qué hora es la marea baja?

—

English: Sometimes when I go to Spain in winter I like to ski with my boyfriend

Spanish: Algunas veces cuando voy a España en invierno me gusta esquiar con mi novio.

—

English: Our apologies viewers, Mark seems to be having some technical difficulties with his in-ear microphone

Spanish: Nuestras disculpas televidentes, Mark está teniendo problemas técnicos con su auricular

—

English: Officials have released a statement expressing their condolences to the victims' families.

Spanish: Los funcionarios han emitido un comunicado en el que expresan sus condolencias a las familias de las víctimas.

—

English: Then when the calls started coming in after the accident, they assumed these were pranks.

Spanish: Luego, cuando comenzaron a llegar las llamadas después del accidente, asumieron que se trataba de bromas

—

English: We'll be keeping you updated on this story as new information becomes available

Spanish: Los mantendremos actualizado sobre esta historia a medida que haya nueva información disponible.

—

English: We now return you to CNN on TV, already in progress.

Spanish: Ahora lo regresamos a CNN en TV, ya en progreso.

—

English: Well Tom, that's an interesting question.

Spanish: Bueno Tom, esa es una pregunta interesante

—

English: She tried to warn police, but they failed to act.

Spanish: Ella trató de advertir a la policía, pero no actuaron.

—

English: Why has it taken so long for first responders to arrive?

Spanish: ¿Por qué ha tardado tanto en llegar el personal de primeros auxilios?

—

English: Witnesses say the car's doors were jammed shut, trapping the kids inside

Spanish: Testigos dicen que las puertas del auto estaban atascadas, atrapando a los niños adentro.

—

English: Firemen and EMTs are still arriving on the scene

Spanish: Los bomberos y los técnicos de emergencias médicas todavía están llegando a la escena

—

English: Fascinating. What happened next?

Spanish: Fascinante. ¿Qué pasó después?

—

English: Well Larry, we've been told the kids were screaming.

Spanish: Bueno Larry, nos han dicho que los niños estaban gritando.

—

English: Sam, is it known how many cars were involved in the accident?

Spanish: Sam, ¿se sabe cuántos autos estuvieron involucrados en el accidente?

—

English: Joseph what can you tell us?

Spanish: Joseph ¿qué puedes decirnos?

—

English: Welcome to the sports section

Spanish: Bienvenidos a la sección de deportes

—

English: Hello and welcome to BCC news. I am Mathew with the latest headlines.

Spanish: Hola y bienvenido a las noticias BCC. Soy Mathew con los últimos titulares

—

English: I am Michelle and here is the top story about the ongoing election campaign

Spanish: Soy Michelle y les traigo las noticias más relevantes sobre la campaña electoral

—

English: Our sources tell us that ebola was first identified in Africa.

Spanish: Nuestras fuentes indican que el ébola fue identificado por primera vez en África.

—

English: Now back to you, Michelle!

Spanish: Volvemos contigo Michelle

—

English: We've got some important breaking news for you tonight.

Spanish: Tenemos noticias muy importantes de última hora esta noche

—

English: The nurses were unprotected, the virus spread without stopping

Spanish: Los enfermeros estaban desprotegidos, el virus infectaba sin detenerse.

—

English: The consequences of the incident were fatal.

Spanish: Las consecuencias del incidente fueron fatales.

—

English: Baseball is a very important sport in America and the Caribbean

Spanish: El béisbol es un deporte muy importante en América y el Caribe

—

STORY-TIME Chapter 6: John and Danny (English)

Danny and John were talking about Cindy but later, they started talking about sports. Danny is a big fan of sports and John is a bit lazy:

John: Do you exercise?

Danny: Yeah, every day. I love sports and gymnastics.

John: Really? That's cool. What sports do you practice?

Danny: Baseball, tennis and golf.

John: Wow! What do you need to practice baseball?

Danny: A lot of practice and enthusiasm.

John: Where do you practice your favourite sport?

Danny: On the baseball field. And what sport are you a fan of?

John: Oh Danny I hate sports. I prefer eating a lot.

Danny: That's bad my friend. You need to lose weight.

STORY-TIME Capítulo 6: John y Danny (Español)

Danny y John estaban hablando de Cindy pero luego empezaron a hablar de deportes. Danny es un gran fanático de los deportes y John es un poco vago:

John: ¿Haces ejercicio?

Danny: Sí, todos los días. Amo los deportes y la gimnasia.

John: ¿De verdad? Eso es genial. ¿Qué deportes practicas?

Danny: Béisbol, tenis y golf

John: ¡Vaya! ¿Qué necesitas para practicar béisbol?

Danny: Mucha práctica y entusiasmo.

John: ¿Dónde practicas tu deporte favorito?

Danny: En el campo de béisbol. ¿Y de qué deporte eres fanático?

John: Oh Danny, odio los deportes. Prefiero comer mucho.

Danny: Eso está mal amigo mío. Necesitas adelgazar.

———

CHAPTER SIX TEST.

1. In the story above, John needs to lose...
A Money
B Time
C Weight
D Love

2. What does "Baseball player" means?

A Jugador de béisbol
B Jugador de tennis
C Jugador de base
D Jugador de básquet

3. How do you say "Latest News" in spanish?

A Últimos avisos
B Últimos servicios
C Noticia falsa
D Últimas noticias

4. In the story above, what does John hate?

A Sports
B Food
C Women
D Money

5. What word means "Breaking News"

A Noticia mentirosa
B Noticia de última hora
C Noticia callejera
D Noticia rota

_____
_____

Answers: 1) c, 2) a, 3) d, 4) a, 5) b.

_____
_____

Part Seven: Romance

Nice, you have completed chapter six and are ready to delve into chapter seven. In this chapter, we are going to cover everything about love. Let's be honest, you want to have some aces under your sleeve when you fight that Spanish speaking partner. This chapter will teach you what you need to impress your crush. Love is in the air, and learning follows. Let's go!

English: I'm having a great time, how about you?

Spanish: La estoy pasando muy bien, ¿y tú?

—

English: Why did you agree to go on this date with me?

Spanish: ¿Por qué accediste a esta cita conmigo?

—

English: Honey, tell me about your family

Spanish: Cariño, háblame de tu familia

—

English: What type of food do you like the most?

Spanish: ¿Qué tipo de comida es la que más te gusta?

—

English: Would you like to have a drink somewhere else?

Spanish: Quieres ir a tomar copas en otro lugar?

—

English: Would you like to go for ice cream?

Spanish: ¿Vamos a tomar un helado?

—

English: I love you too my dear

Spanish: Yo también te amo mi amor

—

English: I love you more than anything in the world!

Spanish: ¡Te amo más que nada en el mundo!

—

English: The best photograph I have, is the one in which I'm smiling because of you.

Spanish: La mejor foto que tengo, es aquella en la cual sonrío por ti.

—

English: It doesn't matter that we're separated by distance, there will always be the same sky to unite us.

Spanish: No importa que nos separe la distancia, siempre habrá un mismo cielo que nos una

—

English: I love you not only because of the way you are, but because of the way I am when I am with you.

Spanish: Te quiero no solo por cómo eres, sino por como soy yo cuando estoy contigo

—

English: It took me an hour to get to know you and just a day to fall in love. But it will take me a whole lifetime to be able to forget you.

Spanish: Tardé una hora en conocerte y solo un día en enamorarme. Pero me llevará toda una vida lograr olvidarte.

—

English: Love me when I least deserve it, because it will be when I need it the most.

Spanish: Ámame cuando menos lo merezca, porque será cuando más lo necesite.

—

English: Love is finding in someone else's happiness our own.

Spanish: Amar es encontrar en la felicidad de otro la propia felicidad

—

English: Love it's not to look at each other, it's to look together towards the same direction.

Spanish: Amar no es mirarse el uno al otro, es mirar juntos en la misma dirección.

—

English: When I was a kid I dreamed of conquering the world, now I realize that you're my world and you have conquered me.

Spanish: Cuando era niño soñaba con conquistar el mundo, ahora me doy cuenta que tu eres mi mundo y me has conquistado.

—

English: This life is mine, but this heart is yours. This smile is mine, but the reason is you.

Spanish: Esta vida es mía, pero este corazón es tuyo. Esta sonrisa es mía, pero la razón eres tú.

—

English: I prefer a minute with you than an eternity without you.

Spanish: Prefiero un minuto contigo a una eternidad sin ti

—

English: Let's go for ice cream!

Spanish: ¡Comamos un helado!

—

English: Will you marry me?

Spanish: ¿Quieres casarte conmigo?

—

English: I love you and I want to be with you everyday

Spanish: Te amo y quiero estar contigo cada día

—

English: I had a wonderful time with you

Spanish: La pasé muy bien contigo

—

English: Jenna can I kiss you? I love you

Spanish: Jenna ¿puedo besarte? Te amo

—

English: Can I buy you dinner tonight?

Spanish: ¿Puedo invitarte a cenar esta noche?

—

English: Are you free on Saturday or Sunday?

Spanish: ¿Estás libre el sábado o el domingo?

—

English: Hello Patricia, you look so beautiful

Spanish: Hola Patricia, luces hermosa

—

English: Did you have a good time tonight?

Spanish: ¿Pasaste una noche increíble?

—

English: What time shall we meet tomorrow?

Spanish: ¿A qué hora podemos salir mañana?

—

English: Let me know when you get home

Spanish: Por favor avísame cuando llegues a tu casa

—

English: Would you like to hang out with me?

Spanish: ¿Te gustaría pasar tiempo conmigo?

—

English: What do you think of this place?

Spanish: ¿Qué piensas sobre este lugar?

—

English: When can I see you again?

Spanish: ¿Cuándo puedo volver a verte?

—

English: I will drive you home

Spanish: Voy a llevarte a tu casa

—

English: Are you free this weekend?

Spanish: ¿Estás libre este fin de semana?

—

English: Nothing truly ever made sense until you came into my life.

Spanish: Nada tenía sentido en mi vida antes de que llegaras a ella

—

English: Thinking of you keeps me awake

Spanish: Pensar en ti me mantiene despierto

—

English: True love stories never end.

Spanish: Las historias de amor verdadero nunca terminan

—

English: All I need is you

Spanish: Tu eres todo lo que necesito

—

English: Close your eyes, fall in love, stay here.

Spanish: Cierra los ojos, enamórate y quédate aquí

—

English: I miss your touch I miss your kiss, I miss every part of your body.

Spanish: Extraño tus caricias, tus besos y cada parte de tu cuerpo.

—

English: Good night, sleep tight, until tomorrow when we see each other again.

Spanish: Buenas noches hasta que nos veamos mañana nuevamente

—

English: Your beautiful eyes are the brightest thing in this world.

Spanish: La cosa más luminosa en este mundo son tus hermosos ojos

—

English: I always want to be with you no matter what, but time shall tell.

Spanish: Siempre quiero estar contigo no importa cuando, pero el tiempo lo dira todo.

—

English: I want you to have a lovely night rest.

Spanish: Quiero que descanses bien esta noche.

—

English: No one can give me the kind of joy you give to me

Spanish: Nadie puede darme la clase de alegría que tú me das

—

English: No matter how far you are from me, I can walk a thousand miles to get to you, queen of my heart

Spanish: No importa lo lejos que estés de mí, puedo caminar miles de millas por ti, reina de mi corazón

—

English: I want to be by your side to comfort you and make you happy

Spanish: Quiero estar a tu lado para hacerte feliz

—

English: I am more tired today because I've been thinking about you all day.

Spanish: Estoy muy cansado hoy porque pasé el día pensando en ti

—

English: I love you my angel. Good night

Spanish: Te amo ángel mío. Buenas noches

—

English: I want you to fall asleep slowly because I am there waiting patiently in your dreams

Spanish: Quiero que duermas lentamente porque estoy esperando que me veas en tus sueños

—

English: I am sending you this cute message and along with it my heart full of love just for you

Spanish: Te envío este mensaje con cariño y con mi corazón lleno de amor para ti

—

English: I still feel some part of me is missing right now

Spanish: Todavía siento que hace falta una parte de mí.

—

English: I don't think sleeping will be possible without me wishing you good night

Spanish: No creo que pueda dormir sin desearte una buena noche

—

English: So go to sleep and forget your worries I will take care of it for you

Spanish: Duérmete y olvida tus preocupaciones, los cuidaré por ti

—

English: Love, you are the reason behind all my joy

Spanish: Amor, eres la razón detrás de toda mi alegría

—

English: You are the best and the cutest

Spanish: Eres lo mejor y lo más tierno

—

English: No one else would have made me feel this way.

Spanish: Nadie me había hecho sentir de esta forma

—

English: You amaze me and you know it.

Spanish: Me sorprendes y lo sabes.

—

English: I want to be your strength.

Spanish: Quiero ser tu fuerza.

—

English: Do you want to be my boyfriend?/girlfriend?

Spanish: ¿Quieres ser mi novio/novia?

—

English: You are my Superman, my buddy in both good and bad times.

Spanish: Eres mi superman, mi amigo en las buenas y en las malas

—

English: You deserve everything I am.

Spanish: Verdaderamente, mereces todo lo que soy

—

English: Can you handle me?

Spanish: ¿Puedes tomar todo de mí?

—

English: The love we share is divine

Spanish: El amor que compartimos es divino

—

English: I love everything about you, your body and soul are perfect

Spanish: Amo todo de ti, tu cuerpo y alma son perfectos

—

English: If you are in my dreams and I am in yours, I will be happy

Spanish: Si estás en mis sueños y yo en los tuyos, seré feliz

—

English: Harry I need to tell you something very important

Spanish: Harry necesito decirte algo muy importante

—

English: Oh I see, Please tell me

Spanish: Oh ya veo. Por favor, dime

—

English: I think we can be a couple. I really like you

Spanish: Yo creo que podemos ser una pareja. Me gustas mucho

—

English: I think you are an angel, you are very pretty and intelligent

Spanish: Creo que eres un ángel, eres muy hermosa e inteligente

—

English: I never thought I will be addicted to someone did way I am to you

Spanish: Nunca pensé que sería adicto a alguien de la manera que estoy tan acostumbrado a ti

—

English: You're the first person who's made this city feel like home

Spanish: Eres la primera persona que hizo sentir esta ciudad como un hogar para mí

—

English: Has anyone ever told you your eyes look like sunflowers?

Spanish: ¿Alguna vez alguien te dijo que tus ojos se ven como girasoles?

—

English: I thought I was having a really great day, then I saw you and got so much better

Spanish: Creía que estaba pasando un día muy bueno pero desde que te vi se volvió mejor

—

English: I've been thinking about you a lot lately and finally worked up the courage to ask if you ever think about me?

Spanish: He pensado en ti recientemente y ahora tengo el coraje de preguntarte si tú piensas en mí

—

English: I'd really like to spend more time with just you.

Spanish: Me gustaría pasar más tiempo contigo

—

English: I just wanted to take a minute and let you know how much you mean to me

Spanish: Yo quería tomar un minuto para decirte cuanto significas para mí

—

STORY-TIME Chapter 7: Tinder (English)

Mark and Lory have met on Tinder, the popular dating application, and they have agreed to have a few beers in a central bar in Barcelona.

Lory: So where are you from?

Mark: From the US, originally. But I lived in Berlin for a few years before moving to Barcelona.

Lory: And how long have you been living here?

Mark: About a year now.

Lory: Do you like it?

Mark: Yeah, I like it a lot! The weather's great, the food is amazing… the only problem is the rent, its ridiculous.

Lory: Yeah. Well, I live with my flatmates. But I have friends who live alone. It's really expensive for them. Anyway, what do you usually do on weekends?

Mark: It depends… sometimes I go to the beach to play volleyball. Sometimes I go out with my friends. Sometimes I just stay at home and watch Netflix.

Lory: That sounds good. So… have you met a lot of girls on Tinder?

Mark: I guess I've met two or three. Nobody I really connected with, though. You?

Lory: I just downloaded it last week, so actually, you're the first guy I've met.

Mark: That's good. So, uh... what kind of relationship are you looking for?

Lory: Oh, you know. I recently broke up with my boyfriend. Now I just wanna have some fun. And then let's see where it takes me!

Mark: Great! Want another beer?

Lory: Sure, why not?

STORY-TIME Capítulo 7: Tinder (Español)

Mark y Lory se han conocido en Tinder, la popular aplicación de coqueteo, y se han reunido para tomarse unas cervezas en un bar céntrico de Barcelona.

Lory: Entonces, ¿de dónde eres?

Mark: Originalmente de Estados Unidos. Pero viví en Berlín unos años antes de trasladarme a Barcelona.

Lory: ¿Y cuánto tiempo llevas viviendo aquí?

Mark: Aproximadamente un año ahora.

Lory: ¿Te gusta?

Mark: ¡Sí, me gusta mucho! Hace buen tiempo, la comida es increíble... el único problema es que los alquileres son ridículamente caros.

Lory: Sí. Bueno, vivo con mis compañeros de piso. Pero tengo amigos que viven solos. Es muy caro para ellos. De todos modos, ¿qué sueles hacer los fines de semana?

Mark: Depende... a veces voy a la playa a jugar al voleibol. A veces salgo con mis amigos. A veces me quedo en casa y veo Netflix.

Lory: Eso suena bien. Entonces... ¿has conocido a muchas chicas en Tinder?

Mark: Supongo que he conocido a dos o tres. Sin embargo, nadie con quien realmente me conecté. ¿Tú?

Lory: Lo descargué la semana pasada, así que, en realidad, eres el primer chico que conozco.

Mark: Eso es bueno. Entonces, eh... ¿qué tipo de relación estás buscando?

Lory: Oh, ya sabes. Recientemente rompí con mi novio. Ahora solo quiero divertirme un poco. ¡Y luego veamos a dónde me lleva esto!

Mark: ¡Genial! ¿Quieres otra cerveza?

Lory: Claro, ¿por qué no?

—

CHAPTER SEVEN TEST.

1. In the story above, Lory and Mark met on...

A Facebook

B Tinder

C Twitter

D Pinterest

2. What does "Date" means?

A Amor

B Comer

C Cupido

D Cita

3. How do you say "Girlfriend" in Spanish?

A Novia

B Novio

C Esposo

D Esposa

4. How do you say "Honey" in Spanish?

A Osito

B Bebé

C Cariño

D Angelito

5. What word means "kissing each other"

A Besarse

B Amarse

C Bañarse

D Dormir juntos

Answers: 1) b, 2) d, 3) a, 4) c, 5) a.

Part Eight: Business

Welcome to chapter eight, you are almost there, but still there's quite a bit to learn. Entrepreneurs, businesses, economy, and making money are all things people enjoy learning. After all, one big reason why people choose to learn Spanish is to immerse themselves in new opportunities with companies native to the tongue. In this chapter, we are going to teach you exactly that, so be ready to learn about the sweet science of making money.

English: Time is money

Spanish: El tiempo es oro

—

English: Harry, how good are you at negotiating?

Spanish: Harry ¿Cuán bueno eres negociando?

—

English: What are some good negotiation tactics?

Spanish: ¿Cuáles son las mejores tácticas de negociación?

—

English: "Business is a combination of war and sport." Do you agree?

Spanish: "Los negocios son la mezcla de la guerra y el deporte" ¿Está usted de acuerdo?

—

English: Do you do negotiations in your work, personal life or while shopping?

Spanish: ¿Negocias en tu trabajo, vida personal o cuando vas de compras?

—

English: What have you had to negotiate for in your life?

Spanish: ¿Qué cosas has tenido que negociar en la vida?

—

English: I think women are better at negotiating.

Spanish: Yo creo que las mujeres son mejores negociando.

—

English: Have you ever worked in another country?

Spanish: ¿Alguna vez has trabajado en un país extranjero?

—

English: If you could choose, where would you like to work abroad?

Spanish: Si pudieras elegir ¿En qué país extranjero te gustaría trabajar?

—

English: What are some cultural differences between your country and foreign countries your company does business with?

Spanish: ¿Cuáles son las diferencias culturales entre tu país y los países con los que tu empresa hace negocios?

—

English: What kinds of crises occur in your workplace?

Spanish: ¿Qué tipo de crisis suceden en tu espacio de trabajo?

—

English: How do you manage crises?

Spanish: ¿Cómo manejas la crisis?

English: What sorts of crisis have affected your economy?

Spanish: ¿Qué tipo de crisis han afectado tu economía?

—

English: What is your back-up plan for a major crisis?

Spanish: ¿Cuál es tu plan de emergencias para cuando venga una crisis mayor?

—

English: What have you learned from past business crisis?

Spanish: ¿Qué has aprendido sobre las crisis de tus negocios?

—

English: How do you feel about giving presentations?

Spanish: ¿Cómo te sientes haciendo exposiciones?

—

English: What makes a bad presentation?

Spanish: ¿Qué hace una mala exposición?

—

English: What qualities make a good manager?

Spanish: ¿Qué cualidades hacen a un buen gerente?

—

English: What is your manager's managing style?

Spanish: ¿Cuál es el estilo en el que gestiona tu jefe?

—

English: How can a manager motivate employees?

Spanish: ¿Cómo puede un gerente motivar a los empleados?

—

English: Are small businesses common in your district?

Spanish: ¿Los negocios pequeños son comunes en tu distrito?

—

English: What challenges do small businesses have in your country?

Spanish: ¿Qué retos poseen los pequeños negocios en tu país?

—

English: What makes a successful small businesses in your city?

Spanish: ¿Qué convierte en exitoso a un pequeño negocio en tu ciudad?

—

English: How can a small business become successful?

Spanish: ¿Cómo se puede volver exitoso un pequeño negocio?

—

English: If you had a small business, what kind would it be?

Spanish: Si tuvieras un pequeño negocio ¿Qué tipo de negocio sería?

—

English: Do you go on business trips at work? Where?

Spanish: ¿Haces viajes de negocios? ¿A dónde?

—

English: What are the disadvantages of business trips?

Spanish: ¿Cuáles son las desventajas de los viajes de negocios?

—

English: What advice do you have for somebody traveling for business?

Spanish: ¿Qué consejo tienes para alguien que viaja por negocios?

—

English: Where would you like to go on a business trip?

Spanish: ¿A dónde te gustaría ir en un viaje de negocios?

—

English: What do you think is the future of business trips?

Spanish: ¿Cuál crees que es el futuro en los viajes de negocios?

—

English: Who exactly is your company's competition?

Spanish: ¿Quién es exactamente la competencia de tu empresa?

—

English: What advantages does your competition have?

Spanish: ¿Qué ventajas posee tu competencia?

—

English: How can your company overcome the competition?

Spanish: ¿Cómo puede tu empresa superar a la competencia?

—

English: How competitive is your industry?

Spanish: ¿Cuán competitivo es tu industria?

—

English: How competitive are you in general?

Spanish: ¿Cuán competitivo eres tú en general?

—

English: Does your company have a contingency plan?

Spanish: ¿Posee tu empresa algún plan de contingencia?

—

English: What is your plan in case you come across a risk?

Spanish: ¿Cuál es tu plan en caso de que exista un riesgo en tu empresa?

—

English: What situation could be a big risk to your company?

Spanish: ¿Qué situación pude ser un riesgo para tu compañía?

—

English: How does your company handle these risks?

Spanish: ¿Cómo lidia tu compañía con esos riesgos?

—

English: What risks does your company come across?

Spanish: ¿Qué riesgos atraviesa tu compañía?

—

English: What is your opinion on investing?

Spanish: ¿Cuál es tu opinión sobre las inversiones?

—

English: What investments do you have?

Spanish: ¿Qué inversiones posees?

—

English: Are you a conservative or risky investor?

Spanish: ¿Eres un inversionista de riesgo o conservador?

—

English: What do you consider to be a bad investment?

Spanish: ¿Qué consideras una mala inversión?

—

English: If you had $100 to invest, what would you do?

Spanish: Si posees 100$ para invertir ¿Qué harías?

—

English: What is your understanding of marketing?

Spanish: ¿Qué entiendes por mercadotecnia?

—

English: What is your company's target market?

Spanish: ¿Cuál es el público objetivo de tu empresa?

—

English: What kind of marketing does your company use?

Spanish: ¿Qué tipo de mercadotecnia usa tu empresa?

—

English: In your opinion what forms of marketing are the most successful?

Spanish: En tu opinion ¿Cuáles formas de mercadotecnia son más exitosas?

—

English: What kind of marketing is successful in your country?

Spanish: ¿Qué tipo de mercadotecnia es exitoso en tu país?

—

English: What is your opinion of consultants?

Spanish: Cuál es tu opinión sobre los consultores?

—

English: What area of advice are you an expert at?

Spanish: ¿En qué área de consejos eres experto?

—

English: Sometimes you need a consultant to tell you the obvious

Spanish: A veces necesitas un consultor para que te diga lo obvio

—

English: Have you ever had any problems with rules and regulations?

Spanish: ¿Alguna vez has tenido problemas con las reglas y regulaciones?

—

English: Why do you think rules and regulations exist?

Spanish: ¿Por qué crees que las reglas existen?

—

English: How do you feel about the regulations at your job?

Spanish: ¿Cómo te sientes con las reglas en tu trabajo?

—

English: What happens if you break any of these rules?

Spanish: ¿Qué sucede si rompes una de esas reglas?

—

English: What rules and regulations exist at your job?

Spanish: ¿Qué reglas y regulaciones existen en tu trabajo?

—

English: The purpose of today's meeting is to discuss ways to improve customer service.

Spanish: El propósito del meeting de hoy es discutir las formas de mejorar el servicio al cliente.

—

English: Let's start with item number one.

Spanish: Comencemos por el punto uno.

—

English: Thank you all for coming at such short notice

Spanish: Gracias a todos por venir con tan poca antelación.

—

English: We have a number of important matters on the agenda today

Spanish: Tenemos un número importante de cosas en la agenda de hoy

—

English: Now that everyone's here, let's get started with today's agenda

Spanish: Ahora que todos están aquí comenzaremos con la agenda de hoy

—

English: It's alright to be less formal.

Spanish: Está bien ser menos formal.

—

English: First, let's talk about how we can use social media

Spanish: Primero, hablemos de cómo podemos usar las redes sociales.

—

English: Excuse me, could you please clarify what you said about the new travel policy?

Spanish: Disculpe, ¿podría aclarar lo que dijo sobre la nueva política de viajes?

—

English: I'm not sure I understand what you mean by...

Spanish: No estoy seguro de entender a qué te refieres con...

—

English: I'm sorry, I don't quite follow...

Spanish: Lo siento, no lo sigo del todo...

—

English: Before we move on, I think we need to look at...

Spanish: Antes de continuar, creo que debemos analizar...

—

English: I'm sorry, but I don't believe we've talked about...

Spanish: Lo siento, pero no creo que hayamos hablado de...

—

English: One minute please, it seems we haven't discussed…

Spanish: Un minuto por favor, parece que no hemos hablado...

—

English: Moving on, let's take a look at item four on the agenda

Spanish: Continuando, echemos un vistazo al punto cuatro de la agenda...

—

English: In summary, we're going to…

Spanish: En resumen, vamos a...

—

English: This is what we've agreed on.

Spanish: Esto es lo que acordamos.

—

English: So we've decided to do that .

Spanish: Así que hemos decidido eso.

—

English: Thank you all for attending.

Spanish: Gracias por asistir .

—

English: The meeting is adjourned.

Spanish: Se levanta la sesión.

—

English: I guess that will be all for today.

Spanish: Supongo que eso será todo por hoy.

—

English: My business is the best option in the market.

Spanish: Mi negocio es la mejor opción del mercado.

—

English: Our resolutions will be fantastic.

Spanish: Nuestras resoluciones serán fantásticas.

—

STORY-TIME Chapter 8: Business (English)

Kim Turner is a sales representative for the company Furry's Pet Supplies. The company sells a wide variety of products for pets including food, cages, leashes, collars, brushes, toys and more. Today, Kim has an appointment with Mr. Wilson, the owner of a large pet shop called Wilson's.

Kim: Good morning, I'm Kim Turner of Furry's Pet Supplies. I have an appointment this morning with Mr. Wilson.

Receptionist: Yes, come in. Mr. Wilson is expecting you.

Mr. Wilson: Hello.

Kim: Good morning, Mr. Wilson. I'm Kim Turner.

Mr. Wilson: Nice to meet you, Mrs. Turner. Come into my office.

Kim: I have seen that you carry some good products in your shop, but I would like to show you our line of products and the competitive prices that we offer.

Mr. Wilson: Yes, I'd like that.

Kim: This is our new catalog. You can see that we offer leashes in a large variety of different materials, colors and lengths.

Mr. Wilson: Yes, they look very nice. Your company is very professional.

STORY-TIME Capítulo 8: Business (Español)

Kim Turner es representante de ventas de Furry's Pet Supplies. La empresa vende una amplia variedad de productos para mascotas, incluidos alimentos, jaulas, correas, collares, cepillos, juguetes y más. Hoy, Kim tiene una cita con el Sr. Wilson, el dueño de una gran tienda de mascotas llamada Wilson's.

Kim: Buenos días, soy Kim Turner de Furry's Pet Supplies. Tengo una cita esta mañana con el Sr. Wilson.

Recepcionista: Sí, pase. El Sr. Wilson lo está esperando.

Sr. Wilson: Hola.

Kim: Buenos días, Sr. Wilson. Soy Kim Turner.

Sr. Wilson: Encantado de conocerla, Sra. Turner. Entre en mi oficina.

Kim: He visto que tiene buenos productos en su tienda, pero me gustaría mostrarle nuestra línea de productos y los precios competitivos que ofrecemos.

Sr. Wilson: Sí, me gustaría.

Kim: Este es nuestro nuevo catálogo. Puede ver que ofrecemos correas en una gran variedad de diferentes materiales, colores y longitudes.

Sr. Wilson: Sí, se ven muy bien. Tu empresa es muy profesional.

CHAPTER EIGHT TEST.

1. In the story above, who is Kim Turner?
A A Nurse
B A Doctor
C A Sales representative
D A Secretary

2. What does "Business" means?
A Negocio
B Fábrica
C Dinero
D Empresario

3. How do you say "Employee" in Spanish?
A Jefe
B Cocinero
C Empleado
D Esposo

4. How do you say "Investment" in Spanish?
A Inversión
B Investo
C Involuntario
D Inalterable

5. What word means "Manager"
A Gerente
B Mesero
C Gestante
D Garantía

Answers: 1) c, 2) a, 3) c, 4) a, 5) a.

Part Nine: Politics

You have advanced very fast! Congratulations! It is safe to say that you are now ready for the big leagues, and by big leagues we mean talking politics. Politics is a very popular topic in every conversation, but it can get technical. We are here to prepare you for this, so rest assured, by the end of this chapter you will know a thing or two about politics and how to express your ideologies in Spanish.

English: Did you vote in the last election?

Spanish: ¿Votó en las últimas elecciones?

—

English: How old were you when you first voted?

Spanish: ¿Qué edad tenía cuando votó por primera vez?

—

English: What is the minimum voting age in your country?

Spanish: ¿Cuál es la edad mínima para votar en su país?

—

English: What type of political system does your country have?

Spanish: ¿Qué tipo de sistema político tiene su país?

—

English: What different types of governments are there?

Spanish: ¿Qué diferentes tipos de gobiernos existen?

—

English: What does an ambassador do?

Spanish: ¿Qué hace un embajador?

—

English: Who appoints an ambassador?

Spanish: ¿Quién nombra al embajador?

—

English: Why is it important to have reliable ambassadors?

Spanish: ¿Por qué es importante tener embajadores fiables?

English: What characteristics should a good ambassador have?

Spanish: ¿Qué características debe tener un buen embajador?

—

English: Who is the mayor of your city?

Spanish: ¿Quién es el alcalde de tu ciudad?

—

English: What are the main political parties in your country?

Spanish: ¿Cuáles son los principales partidos políticos de su país?

—

English: How do you decide how you will vote?

Spanish: ¿Cómo decides cómo vas a votar?

—

English: Who represents you in your local and national government?

Spanish: ¿Quién lo representa en su gobierno local y nacional?

—

English: How long is the term of elected officials in your country?

Spanish: ¿Cuánto tiempo dura el mandato de los funcionarios electos en su país?

—

English: Which party is now in power in your country?

Spanish: ¿Qué partido está ahora en el poder en su país?

—

English: When were they elected?

Spanish: ¿Cuándo fueron elegidos?

—

English: Who is the leader of this party?

Spanish: ¿Quién es el líder de este partido?

—

English: How can we get more people to vote?

Spanish: ¿Cómo podemos conseguir que más gente vote?

—

English: Is voting an important responsibility of a citizen?

Spanish: ¿Votar es una responsabilidad importante de un ciudadano?

—

English: Why do you think voting is important?

Spanish: ¿Por qué cree que votar es importante?

—

English: How are elections financed?

Spanish: ¿Cómo se financian las elecciones?

—

English: Do you think too much money is spent on campaigns?

Spanish: ¿Crees que se gasta demasiado dinero en campañas?

—

English: How can campaigns be better organized?

Spanish: ¿Cómo se pueden organizar mejor las campañas?

—

English: How could elections be more representative?

Spanish: ¿Cómo podrían las elecciones ser más representativas?

—

English: Should voting be compulsory?

Spanish: ¿Debería ser obligatorio votar?

—

English: What is your opinion about actors or actresses who run for a position in politics?

Spanish: ¿Cuál es su opinión sobre los actores o actrices que se postulan para un puesto en política?

—

English: Would you vote for an actor or actress who campaigns for a government position?

Spanish: ¿Votaría por un actor o actriz que hace campaña para un puesto en el gobierno?

—

English: What type of political system governs your country?

Spanish: ¿Qué tipo de sistema político gobierna en su país?

—

English: What are some different types of governments?

Spanish: ¿Cuáles son algunos tipos diferentes de gobiernos?

—

English: What are the main political parties in the country where you live?

Spanish: ¿Cuáles son los principales partidos políticos del país donde vives?

—

English: Which politicians represent you in local and national government?

Spanish: ¿Qué políticos te representan en el gobierno local y nacional?

—

English: Can you name the President of the United States?

Spanish: ¿Puede nombrar al presidente de los Estados Unidos?

—

English: Which party is in power at the moment in your country?

Spanish: ¿Qué partido está en el poder en este momento en su país?

—

English: When were they elected?

Spanish: ¿Cuándo fueron elegidos?

—

English: Who is the leader of this party?

Spanish: ¿Quién es el líder de este partido?

—

English: Do you agree with most of their policies?

Spanish: ¿Está de acuerdo con la mayoría de sus políticas?

—

English: Have your political views changed much during your lifetime?

Spanish: ¿Han cambiado mucho tus opiniones políticas durante su vida?

—

English: What are the benefits and drawbacks of being an EU member?

Spanish: ¿Cuáles son las ventajas y las desventajas de ser miembro de la UE?

—

English: Do you think that every future politician should be vetted for security reasons?

Spanish: ¿Cree que todos los futuros políticos deberían ser examinados por razones de seguridad?

—

English: Who is the most controversial politician in your country?

Spanish: ¿Quién es el político más polémico de su país?

—

English: Politics are the best way to solve humanitarian situations.

Spanish: Las políticas son la mejor forma de resolver los problemas humanitarios.

—

English: Politicians are people's employees.

Spanish: Los politicos son empleados del pueblo.

—

English: Nobody can predict the future but the law is the people's key.

Spanish: Nadie puede predecir el futuro pero la ley es la llave del pueblo.

—

English: A leader can be cruel or humble but never stupid.

Spanish: Un líder puede ser cruel o humilde pero nunca estúpido.

—

English: If public reaction is favorable, the politician takes credit for it; if not, the idea dies quickly.

Spanish: Si la reacción del público es favorable, el político se atribuye el mérito; si no, la idea muere rápidamente.

—

English: When politicians traveled by train, small towns were called whistle-stops.

Spanish: Cuando los políticos viajaban en tren, a los pueblos pequeños se les llamaba paradas de emergencia.

—

English: Law is a rule or regulation established by the government.

Spanish: La ley es una regla o reglamento establecido por el gobierno.

—

English: Election is the process of voting for a candidate or representative.

Spanish: La elección es el proceso de votar por un candidato o representante.

—

English: All the people who can vote in an election are an electorate.

Spanish: Todas las personas que pueden votar en una elección son electorado.

—

English: Government is a political body that exercises authority over a nation or state and has the power to make and enforce laws.

Spanish: El gobierno es un cuerpo político que ejerce autoridad sobre una nación o estado y tiene el poder de hacer y hacer cumplir las leyes.

—

English: Grass roots are ordinary people in a society, as opposed to those who are in power.

Spanish: Las bases son personas comunes en una sociedad, a diferencia de los que están en el poder.

—

English: Hustings are the political activities, meetings and speeches that happen before an election.

Spanish: Los homenajes son las actividades políticas, reuniones y discursos que ocurren antes de una elección.

—

English: Incumbent is a person currently holding an official position.

Spanish: El incumbente es una persona que actualmente ocupa un cargo oficial.

—

English: Monarchy is the system of government in which the head of state is a king or a queen.

Spanish: La monarquía es el sistema de gobierno en el que el jefe de estado es un rey o una reina.

—

English: Nominee is the person chosen by a political party to run for election.

Spanish: Nominado es la persona elegida por un partido político para presentarse a las elecciones.

—

English: Opposition is the political party or parties opposing the government.

Spanish: La oposición es el partido o partidos políticos que se oponen al gobierno.

—

English: Political asylum is a protection given by a State to a person who has left their own country because they oppose its government.

Spanish: El asilo político es una protección otorgada por un Estado a una persona que ha abandonado su propio país porque se opone a su gobierno.

—

English: Political party is a political organization with stated beliefs, aims and policies that puts forward candidates in elections.

Spanish: El partido político es una organización política con creencias, objetivos y políticas declaradas que presenta candidatos en las elecciones.

—

English: Politician is a person who has been elected and works professionally in politics.

Spanish: Político es una persona que ha sido elegida y trabaja profesionalmente en política.

—

English: Politics are the ideas and activities associated with the governing of a country, region, city, etc.

Spanish: La política son las ideas y actividades asociadas con el gobierno de un país, región, ciudad, etc.

—

English: A Republic is a system of government in which power is held by elected representatives and an elected president.

Spanish: Una República es un sistema de gobierno en el que el poder está en manos de representantes electos y un presidente electo.

—

English: To run for election is to be a candidate in an election.

Spanish: Presentarse a las elecciones es ser candidato en una elección.

—

English: A turnout is the number of people who go to vote in an election.

Spanish: La participación es el número de personas que van a votar en una elección.

—

English: You vote to choose a candidate in an election.

Spanish: Votar es elegir un candidato en una elección.

—

English: Every vote is important. One of them can make the difference.

Spanish: Cada voto es importante. Uno de ellos puede hacer la diferencia.

—

English: There are good and bad political parties.

Spanish: Hay buenos y malos partidos políticos

—

English: A divided country is a weak country.

Spanish: Un país dividido es un país débil.

—

English: The antidote for corruption is prison.

Spanish: El antídoto para los corruptos es la cárcel.

—

English: There is no nation if there is no law.

Spanish: No hay nación sin ley.

—

English: The constitution is a citizen's best weapon.

Spanish: La constitución es la mejor arma para un ciudadano.

—

English: Some people think war is a good solution.

Spanish: Algunas personas creen que la guerra es una buena solución.

—

English: Sometimes politicians are wolves.

Spanish: Algunas veces los políticos son lobos.

—

English: Being perfect is impossible but not in democracy.

Spanish: Ser perfecto es imposible pero no en democracia.

—

English: Some rules were written by stupid leaders.

Spanish: Algunas reglas fueron escritas por líderes estúpidos.

—

English: A nation's horizon is eternal.

Spanish: El horizonte de una nación es eterno.

—

STORY-TIME Chapter 9: Students (English)

Maria and Jack are the new student presidents of Ohio. They studied together since kindergarten, they loved politics and are now fellow party members. But sometimes they do not agree with each other and arguments ensue.

Maria: I don't agree with you! I think we should ban school uniforms

Jack: No way, uniforms help us avoid inequality

Maria: That sounds very socialist! I think you're a bit unorthodox.

Jack: It's not about that. You're overreacting.

Maria: Exaggerating? You are in favor of uniforms

Jack: It's just an opinion, you must learn to respect other points of view

Maria: I'm sorry friend but you're wrong

Jack: Then we must call a vote.

Maria: That is absurd

Jack: No! That is called democracy, not socialism.

STORY-TIME Capítulo 9: Estudiantes (Español)

Maria y Jack son los nuevos presidentes estudiantiles de Ohio. Ambos estudiaron juntos desde el jardín de infancia, les encantaba la política y ahora eran compañeros de partido. Pero a veces no se ponían de acuerdo y comenzaban a discutir.

Maria: ¡No estoy de acuerdo contigo! Yo creo que debemos prohibir los uniformes escolares.

Jack: De ninguna manera, los uniformes nos ayudan a evitar la desigualdad.

Maria: ¡Eso suena muy socialista! Creo que eres un poco ortodoxo.

Jack: No se trata de eso. Estás exagerando.

Maria: ¿Exagerando? Tú estás a favor de los uniformes.

Jack: Es solo una opinion, debes aprender a respetar otros puntos de vista.

Maria: Lo siento amigo pero estás equivocado.

Jack: Entonces debemos convocar una votación.

Maria: Eso es absurdo.

Jack: ¡No! Eso se llama democracia, no socialismo.

—

CHAPTER NINE TEST.

1. In the story above, according to Maria, Jack is a...

A Dictador

B Democrat

C Liberal

D Socialist

2. What does "Mayor" means?
A Senador
B Alcalde
C Ministro
D Empresario

3. How do you say "Politics" in Spanish?
A Política
B Polígrafo
C Poligrafía
D Poster

4. How do you say "Senate" in Spanish?
A Cenar
B Senado
C Sena
D Séneca

5. What word means "Political Party"
A Político de fiesta
B Político corrupto
C Partido político
D Partido de fútbol

_____

_____

Answers: 1) D, 2) B, 3) A, 4) B, 5) C.

_____

_____

Part Ten: Entertainment

Politics is history, the next chapter is a mystery. Just kidding, we are going to tell you exactly what you're going to learn. It's time for some entertainment. You will learn how to talk show business. At the end of this chapter, you will be able to gossip with your friend about your favorite celebrity. Practice is key, so master every phrase before jumping to the next.

English: The hotel is famous for its entertainment.

Spanish: El hotel es famoso por su entretenimiento.

—

English: The town provides a wide choice of entertainment.

Spanish: La ciudad ofrece una amplia variedad de entretenimiento.

—

English: Ed Sheeran is having a concert tonight. We should go.

Spanish: Ed Sheeran tendrá un concierto esta noche. Deberíamos ir.

—

English: There's something charmingly old-fashioned about his brand of entertainment.

Spanish: Hay algo encantadoramente anticuado en su estilo de entretenimiento.

—

English: The resort offers endless possibilities for entertainment.

Spanish: El complejo ofrece infinitas posibilidades de entretenimiento.

—

English: Brad Pitt is a famous Hollywood star.

Spanish: Brad Pitt es una famosa estrella de Hollywood.

—

English: Soaps like "Neighbors" are pure entertainment and there is nothing wrong with that.

Spanish: Telenovelas como "Neighbors" son puro entretenimiento y no hay nada de malo en eso.

—

English: This was some first class entertainment.

Spanish: Esto fue un entretenimiento de primera clase.

—

English: The entertainment was good clean fun for the whole family

Spanish: El entretenimiento fue muy divertido para toda la familia.

—

English: Stars of the entertainment world turned out to celebrate his 40th year in show business.

Spanish: Estrellas del mundo del entretenimiento celebraron sus 40 años en el mundo del espectáculo.

—

English: Cinemas are now close due to the pandemic.

Spanish: Los cines están cerrados por la pandemia.

—

English: There will be live entertainment throughout the day.

Spanish: Habrá entretenimiento en vivo durante todo el día.

—

English: Gambling is a form of entertainment than can be very addicting.

Spanish: Los juego de azar son una forma de entretenimiento que pueden resultar ser muy adictivas.

—

English: The entertainment was provided by a folk band.

Spanish: El entretenimiento estuvo a cargo de una banda folclórica.

—

English: There's not much in the way of entertainment in this town – just the cinema and a couple of pubs.

Spanish: No hay mucho entretenimiento en esta ciudad, solo el cine y un par de bares.

—

English: They lead the field in home entertainment systems.

Spanish: Lideran el campo de los sistemas de entretenimiento en el hogar.

—

English: I miss the theaters so much.

Spanish: Extraño tanto el cine.

—

English: They organized an evening's entertainment for exclusive customers.

Spanish: Organizaron una velada de entretenimiento para clientes privilegiados.

—

English: One movie movie is art, the other is pure trash.

Spanish: Una película es arte, la otra es pura basura.

—

English: She recited a long poem at the New Year's Eve party.

Spanish: Recitó un largo poema en el espectáculo de Año Nuevo.

—

English: The amusement park will fill a void in this town, which has little entertainment for children.

Spanish: El parque de atracciones llenará un vacío en este pueblo, que tiene poco entretenimiento para los niños.

—

English: Would you classify her novels as serious literature?

Spanish: ¿Clasificaría sus novelas como literatura seria?

—

English: Television has displaced film as our country's most popular form of entertainment.

Spanish: La televisión ha desplazado al cine como la forma de entretenimiento más popular de nuestro país.

—

English: Many famous celebrities are not as happy as they seem.

Spanish: Muchas famosas celebridades no son tan felices como parecen.

—

English: Social media is the new Hollywood.

Spanish: Las redes sociales son el nuevo Hollywood.

—

English: In his day, Shakespeare was low-brow entertainment for the common class.

Spanish: En su día, Shakespeare era un entretenimiento de baja categoría para la clase común.

—

English: Numerous institutions contribute to the entertainment of visitors.

Spanish: Numerosas instituciones contribuyen al entretenimiento de los visitantes.

—

English: She works in the entertainment industry.

Spanish: Ella trabaja en la industria del entretenimiento.

—

English: There is a huge entertainment center downtown.

Spanish: Hay un enorme centro de entretenimiento en el centro.

—

English: This show has a high entertainment value.

Spanish: Este espectáculo tiene un alto valor de entretenimiento.

—

English: They have an expensive home entertainment system.

Spanish: Tienen un costoso sistema de entretenimiento en casa.

—

English: This hotel provides a lot of entertainment choices.

Spanish: Este hotel ofrece muchas opciones de entretenimiento.

—

English: I enjoy live entertainment.

Spanish: Disfruto del entretenimiento en vivo.

—

English: This movie is good entertainment.

Spanish: Esta película es un buen entretenimiento.

—

English: Live entertainment is exciting.

Spanish: El entretenimiento en vivo es emocionante.

—

English: There is nightly entertainment on the cruise.

Spanish: Hay entretenimiento nocturno en el crucero.

—

English: She is looking for family entertainment on television.

Spanish: Busca entretenimiento familiar en la televisión.

—

English: The theater also produces a highly successful pantomime that brings festive entertainment to thousands of families each year.

Spanish: El teatro también produce una pantomima de gran éxito que trae entretenimiento festivo a miles de familias cada año

—

English: Here he worked in domestic, commercial and entertainment fields, including the planning of amusement parks.

Spanish: Aquí trabajó en los campos doméstico, comercial y de entretenimiento, incluida la planificación de parques de atracciones.

—

English: Justin Bieber and Jesus Christ are the most famous stars of all time.

Spanish: Justin Bieber y Jesucristo son las estrellas más famosas de todos los tiempos.

—

English: Selena Gómez and Demi Lovato, although they are no longer friends, have many things in common.

Spanish: Selena Gómez y Demi Lovato aunque ya no son amigas, tienen cosas en común.

—

English: Rock music will never go out of style.

Spanish: La música del rock nunca pasará de moda.

—

English: When the stars lose their humility they lose everything.

Spanish: Cuando las estrellas pierden su humildad lo pierden todo.

—

English: Fans make the stars.

Spanish: Los fanáticos hacen a las grandes estrellas.

—

English: There is no show without crazy fans.

Spanish: No existe farándula sin fanáticos alocados.

—

English: In show business anything can happen.

Spanish: En el mundo del espectáculo todo puede suceder.

—

English: When you least expect it, a superstar does something stupid.

Spanish: Cuando menos lo esperas, una super estrella hace algo estúpido

—

English: The press has destroyed the careers of many great artists.

Spanish: La prensa ha destruido la carrera de muchos grandes artistas.

—

English: Many have talent to be stars but they do not have consistency.

Spanish: Muchos tienen talento para ser estrellas pero no tienen la consistencia.

—

English: Many stars have lost their careers to drugs.

Spanish: Muchas estrellas han perdido su carrera por el uso de drogas.

—

English: When fame comes, fortune follows.

Spanish: Cuando llega la fama, llega la fortuna.

—

English: The entertainment business handles a lot of money

Spanish: El negocio del entretenimiento maneja mucho dinero

—

English: Being different can make you a big star.

Spanish: Ser diferente puede convertirte en una gran estrella.

—

English: Getting noticed on TV can make you very rich.

Spanish: Llamar la atención en la televisión puede hacerte muy rico.

—

English: There is no luck, artists build their own future.

Spanish: No existe la suerte, los artistas construyen su propio futuro.

—

English: Being Madonna is not the same as working at Walmart

Spanish: No es lo mismo ser Madonna que trabajar en Walmart

—

English: Hollywood can be very cruel, but can also be very glorious.

Spanish: Hollywood puede ser muy cruel pero también puede ser la gloria.

—

English: Only the big stars know how to shine

Spanish: Solo las grandes estrellas saben brillar

—

English: Superstars are not role models

Spanish: Las super estrellas no son modelos a seguir

—

English: Luck doesn't exist in show business.

Spanish: No existe la suerte en el mundo del espectáculo

—

English: Some people are born to be superstars

Spanish: Algunas personas nacen para ser super estrellas

—

English: Superstars are icons of fashion and style

Spanish: Las super estrellas son iconos de la moda y del estilo

—

English: Miley Cyrus was first a Disney star and then an icon of sexual freedom

Spanish: Miley Cyrus primero fue estrella Disney y luego un ícono de libertad sexual

—

English: Fashion crimes are common in stars

Spanish: Los crímenes de la moda son comunes en las estrellas

—

English: Living in Bel Air is not the same as living in the suburbs

Spanish: No es lo mismo vivir en Bel Air que en los suburbios

—

English: Every superstar has loyal fans by their side

Spanish: Cada super estrella tiene fanáticos fieles a su lado

—

English: Sometimes superstars get lonely

Spanish: A veces las super estrellas se sienten solos

—

STORY-TIME Chapter 10: Gossip Girls (English)

Anne and Marie are best friends and love Justin Bieber. When they were teenagers they went to several of his concerts. Now, Justin Bieber is in Madrid and they want to meet him in person.

Anne: I can't believe it! Justin Bieber is in Madrid.

Marie: We have to find him. Surely he is in Marta's restaurant.

Anne: It's Justin Bieber, he must be in a nightclub. Not eating sandwiches.

Marie: It's true. What are we going to do?

Anne: I don't know but I want to meet him, he is the most handsome man in the world.

Marie: I'm going to marry him.

Anne: Never! He doesn't like blondes.

Marie: How do you know that?

Anne: Obviously, all of his girlfriends have been redheads.

Marie: You say that because you are a redhead.

STORY-TIME Capítulo 10: Chismosas (Español)

Anne y Marie son mejores amigas y aman a Justin Bieber. Cuando eran adolescentes fueron a varios de sus conciertos. Ahora Justin Bieber está en Madrid y ellas desean conocerlo en persona.

Anne: ¡No lo puedo creer! Justin Bieber está en Madrid.

Marie: Tenemos que encontrarlo. Seguramente está en el restaurante de Marta.

Anne: Es Justin Bieber, debe estar en algún club nocturno. No comiendo sándwiches.

Marie: Es cierto. ¿Qué vamos a hacer?

Anne: No lo sé pero quiero conocerlo, él es el hombre más guapo del mundo.

Marie: Yo me voy a casar con él.

Anne: ¡Nunca! A él no le gustan las mujeres rubias

Marie: ¿Cómo sabes eso?

Anne: Es obvio, todas sus novias han sido pelirrojas.

Marie: Eso lo dices porque tú eres pelirroja.

—

CHAPTER TEN TEST.

1. In the story above, ¿Who's Justin Bieber?
A) A superstar
B) A taxi driver
C) A doctor
D) A fireman

2. What does "celebrity" means?

A Celebridad

B Célibe

C Cereza

D Cena

3. How do you say "Show" in Spanish?

A Espectacular

B España

C Espectáculo

D Espectador

4. How do you say "Singer" in Spanish?

A Actor

B Canción

C Cántico

D Cantante

5. What word means "Show Business"

A Negocio

B Espectáculo

C Presentación

D Celebridad

Answers: 1) A, 2) A, 3) C, 4) D, 5) B.

Part Eleven: Job Interviews

Way to go! You have now reached the eleventh chapter of this book. Let's be honest, some of you are learning Spanish because you want to take that next step professionally. This chapter is all about job interviews and business. You will learn how to conduct yourself in one and maybe land that dream job you ever wanted. Remember, practice before jumping to the next chapter.

English: Tell me, why exactly do you want this job? You know the hours are very long, don't you?

Spanish: Dígame ¿Por qué quiere este trabajo exactamente? Sabe que los horarios son muy largos, ¿no?

—

English: Yes, but that doesn't bother me. I think it's a terrific opportunity to progress in my career.

Spanish: Sí, pero eso no me importa. Creo que es una magnífica oportunidad para progresar laboralmente.

—

English: And why do you think we should hire you?

Spanish: ¿Y por qué cree que deberíamos contratarlo?

—

English: I'll bring my experience and great enthusiasm.

Spanish: Puedo aportar mi experiencia y gran entusiasmo.

—

English: Good, we'll look over your CV and then let you know our decision.

Spanish: Muy bien, estudiaremos su currículo y ya le comunicaremos nuestra decisión.

—

English: I'll wait for your call. See you later, thanks for the coffee!

Spanish: Esperaré su llamada. Hasta luego, ¡gracias por el café!

—

English: I need to find a job. How much is the pay?

Spanish: Tengo que buscar un trabajo. ¿Cuánto es el sueldo?

—

English: What do you do for a living?

Spanish: ¿A qué te dedicas?

—

English: You could always get a job at McDonald's

Spanish: Siempre podrías pillarte un trabajo en el McDonald's.

—

English: What position did you have in your old company?

Spanish: ¿Qué puesto ocupaste en tu última empresa?

—

English: What were your greatest achievements in your last job?

Spanish: ¿Cuáles fueron tus mayores logros en tu último trabajo?

—

English: What type of contract is it?

Spanish: ¿Qué tipo de contrato es?

—

English: What's the salary?

Spanish: ¿Cuál es el sueldo?

—

English: Could you tell me about yourself, your experience or knowledge in…?

Spanish: ¿Me podría hablar de usted, su experiencia o conocimientos en…?

—

English: In your opinion, what are your greatest strengths and weaknesses?

Spanish: En tu opinión, ¿cuáles consideras que son tus fortalezas y debilidades?

—

English: What do you know about our company?

Spanish: ¿Qué sabe sobre nuestra empresa?

—

English: Why do you want to change your job?

Spanish: ¿Por qué quieres cambiar de trabajo?

—

English: How do you see yourself in five years?

Spanish: ¿Dónde te ves en cinco años?

—

English: What is your salary expectation?

Spanish: ¿Cuál es su aspiración salarial?

—

English: Do you think that you are the right person for this job?

Spanish: ¿Cree que sea la persona indicada para este trabajo?

—

English: What languages do you speak, and at what level?

Spanish: ¿Qué idiomas habla, y qué nivel tiene?

—

English: What are your goals for the future?

Spanish: ¿Qué metas tiene para el futuro?

—

English: When could you join the company?

Spanish: ¿Cuándo podría incorporarse a la empresa?

—

English: I learned about this company through social network.

Spanish: Conocí a la empresa a través de las redes sociales.

—

English: I worked in the area of...

Spanish: Trabajé en el área de...

—

English: Me veo trabajando y prosperando en...

Spanish: I see myself working and prospering in...

—

English: I see myself assuming and facing new challenges.

Spanish: Me veo asumiendo y enfrentando nuevos retos.

—

English: I'm sure the company pays a fair salary, according to the worker's experience.

Spanish: Estoy seguro que la empresa paga un sueldo justo de acorde a la experiencia del trabajador.

—

English: I am prepared to face changes, and willing to continue working on professionalizing myself.

Spanish: Estoy preparado para afrontar cambios, y dispuesto a seguir trabajando en profesionalizarme.

—

English: I'd like to begin working when…

Spanish: Me gustaría comenzar a trabajar cuando…

—

English: I'm bilingual, I write and speak French and Spanish.

Spanish: Soy bilingüe, escribo y hablo Francés y Español.

—

English: Extra month's salary.

Spanish: El pago extra.

—

English: You've earned yourself a promotion.

Spanish: Se ha ganado usted un ascenso.

—

English: I've had a pay rise.

Spanish: Me han subido el sueldo.

—

English: Apply for a job.

Spanish: Solicitar un trabajo.

—

English: I've applied for a job as a waiter.

Spanish: He solicitado un trabajo de camarero.

—

English: To leave university, to graduate.

Spanish: Egresar de la universidad.

—

English: How do you feel about job interviews?

Spanish: ¿Cómo te sientes con las entrevistas de trabajo?

—

English: What is the most important part of a job interview?

Spanish: ¿Cuál es la parte más importante en una entrevista de trabajo?

—

English: What advice do you have for a successful interview?

Spanish: ¿Qué consejo tienes para una entrevista exitosa?

—

English: What questions are common in job interviews in your country?

Spanish: ¿Qué preguntas son comm.unes en las entrevistas de trabajo de tu país?

—

English: What was the worst interview you have ever had?

Spanish: ¿Cuál ha sido la peor entrevista de trabajo que has tenido?

—

English: What is your definition of a leader?

Spanish: ¿Cuál es tu definición de líder?

—

English: What makes you an excellent leader?

Spanish: ¿Qué te convierte en un gran líder?

—

English: How is the leadership in your country?

Spanish: ¿Cómo es el liderazgo en tu país?

—

English: Describe the best leader you have worked for.

Spanish: Describe al major líder para el que trabajaste,

—

English: How good of a leader do you believe you are?

Spanish: ¿Cuán buen líder crees que eres?

—

English: What is often discussed at your meetings?

Spanish: ¿Qué discusiones tienen en las conferencias?

—

English: How often do you have meetings at work?

Spanish: ¿Cuántas veces tienes conferencias en el trabajo?

—

English: Do you like meetings at work?

Spanish: ¿Te gustan las conferencias de trabajo?

—

English: What are the disadvantages to having meetings?

Spanish: ¿Cuáles son las desventajas de tener conferencias?

—

English: Have you ever been fired?

Spanish: ¿Alguna vez ha sido despedido?

—

English: How does one get fire at your job?

Spanish: ¿Cómo se despide a alguien en tu trabajo?

—

English: Have you ever had to fire anyone?

Spanish: ¿Alguna vez ha tenido que despedir a alguien?

—

English: How can you prevent getting fired?

Spanish: ¿Cómo puede evitar que lo despidan?

—

English: If you were fired, what would you do?

Spanish: Si te despidieran, ¿qué harías?

—

English: Do you have performance reviews in your company? How often?

Spanish: ¿Tiene evaluaciones de desempeño en su empresa? ¿Con qué frecuencia?

—

English: How do you feel about them?

Spanish: ¿Cómo te sientes de ellos?

—

English: What do your performance reviews cover?

Spanish: ¿Qué cubren tus evaluaciones de desempeño?

—

English: How important do you think feedbacks are?

Spanish: ¿Qué importancia crees que tienen las valoraciones?

English: What happens if you have a good/bad appraisal?

Spanish: ¿Qué pasa si tienes una valoración buena / mala?

—

English: How do you feel about feedback about yourself?

Spanish: ¿Qué opinas de los comentarios sobre ti mismo?

—

English: What is the retirement age in your country?

Spanish: ¿Cuál es la edad de jubilación en tu país?

—

English: What do people in your country usually do once they are retired?

Spanish: ¿Qué suele hacer la gente de tu país una vez jubilada?

—

English: Where do retired people usually live in your country?

Spanish: ¿Dónde viven habitualmente los jubilados en tu país?

—

English: What are the advantages/disadvantages to retirement?

Spanish: ¿Cuáles son las ventajas / desventajas de la jubilación?

—

English: What do you think you will do when you retire?

Spanish: ¿Qué crees que harás cuando te jubiles?

—

English: What work experience do you have?

Spanish: ¿Qué experiencia laboral tienes?

—

English: How did you like your previous work?

Spanish: ¿Qué le pareció su trabajo anterior?

—

English: What can you gain from work experience?

Spanish: ¿Qué puedes ganar con la experiencia laboral?

—

English: What have you learned from your work experience?

Spanish: ¿Qué has aprendido de tu experiencia laboral?

—

English: What have you learned about yourself?

Spanish: ¿Qué has aprendido sobre ti mismo?

—

English: What do you think about your colleagues?

Spanish: ¿Qué opinas de tus compañeros?

—

English: What are some common problems with colleagues?

Spanish: ¿Cuáles son algunos problemas comunes con los colegas?

—

English: Have you ever had any challenging situations with your colleagues?

Spanish: ¿Ha tenido alguna vez situaciones desafiantes con tus colegas?

—

English: Do you spend time with your colleagues outside of work?

Spanish: ¿Pasa tiempo con sus colegas fuera del trabajo?

—

English: Who is your favorite colleague? Why?

Spanish: ¿Quién es tu colega favorito? ¿Por qué?

—

English: What does it take to get a raise at your job?

Spanish: ¿Qué se necesita para obtener un aumento en su trabajo?

English: What advice do you have for someone who wants a raise?

Spanish: ¿Qué consejo le daría a alguien que quiera un aumento?

—

English: Do you think raises are important? Why?

Spanish: ¿Crees que los aumentos son importantes? ¿Por qué?

—

STORY-TIME Chapter 11: Job Interview (English)

Interviewer: Welcome to ABC Controls, Shaun. I am Blake.

Interviewee: Hello, it's nice to meet you.

Interviewer: Nice to meet you too, how are you doing today?

Interviewee: I am doing well, and yourself?

Interviewer: Great, thanks. I hope we didn't keep you waiting for long.

Interviewee: No, I had the chance to talk to one of your engineers while waiting.

Interviewer: That's good. Shaun, shall we start?

Interviewee: Yeah, sure.

Interviewer: First of all, let me introduce myself. I am the manager of our engineering department here and we have an open position. We have been interviewing applicants to fill the position as quickly as possible.

Interviewee: Yes sir, I read about the position on your website, and I think I am a good fit.

Interviewer: We currently have several ongoing projects and the team is working hard. We are hoping to keep you busy for a long time.

STORY-TIME Capítulo 11: Entrevista de trabajo (Español)

Entrevistador: Bienvenido a ABC Controls, Shaun. Yo soy Blake.

Entrevistado: Hola, es un gusto conocerte.

Entrevistador: Encantado de conocerte también, ¿cómo estás?

Entrevistado: Estoy bien, ¿y tú?

Entrevistador: Genial, gracias. Espero que no te hayamos hecho esperar mucho.

Entrevistado: No, tuve la oportunidad de hablar con uno de sus ingenieros mientras esperaba.

Entrevistador: Eso es bueno. Shaun, ¿empezamos?

Entrevistado: Sí, claro.

Entrevistador: En primer lugar, permítame presentarme. Soy el gerente de nuestro departamento de ingeniería aquí y tenemos un puesto vacante, por lo que hemos estado entrevistando candidatos para cubrir el puesto lo más rápido posible.

Entrevistado: Sí señor, leí sobre el puesto en su sitio web y creo que encajo bien.

Entrevistador: Actualmente tenemos varios proyectos en curso y el equipo está trabajando duro. Esperamos mantenernos ocupados durante mucho tiempo.

CHAPTER ELEVEN TEST.

1. How are job interviews?

A Informal

B Formal

C Divertidas

D Estupidas

2. What does "Gerente" means?

A Singer

B Manager

C Taxi driver

D Policeman

3. How do you say "Interview" in Spanish?

A Interno

B Internista

C Entrevista

D Inactivo

4. How do you say "Boss" in Spanish?

A Jefe

B Carnicero

C Empleado

D Cantante

5. What word means "Office"

A Oficial

B Oficio

C Casa

D Oficina

Answers: 1) B, 2) B, 3) C, 4) A, 5) D.

Part Twelve: Family

Hello student! Welcome to the last chapter! The journey has been long but we hope you've find it rewarding. You can pretty much go to any Spanish speaking country now and defend yourself against locals, speaking their own tongue. However, now we are going to teach you about the most important thing in your life: family. Hop on board and welcome to the final chapter.

English: I come from a small family.

Spanish: Vengo de una familia pequeña.

—

English: I look like my Dad. We both have blue eyes and blonde hair.

Spanish: Me parezco a mi papá. Los dos tenemos los ojos azules y el cabello rubio.

—

English: I'm very different from my mom. She is talkative and doesn't like to wait for anything, but I'm very shy and patient.

Spanish: Soy muy diferente de mi mamá. Ella es muy habladora y no le gusta esperar por nada, pero yo soy muy tímida y paciente.

—

English: My sister likes staying at home and cooking, but I prefer gardening and outdoor activities.

Spanish: A mi hermana le gusta estar en casa y cocinar, pero yo prefiero la jardinería y las actividades al aire libre.

—

English: My brother enjoys playing sports, but I prefer reading and watching movies.

Spanish: A mi hermano le encantan los deportes, pero yo prefiero leer y ver películas.

—

English: We always have lunch together on weekends. Sometimes we go away for the weekend.

Spanish: Siempre comemos juntos durante los fines de semana. Algunas veces nos vamos fuera por el fin de semana.

—

English: We don't see each other very often, but I try to call my parents once a week.

Spanish: No nos vemos muy a menudo, pero intento llamar a mis papás una vez a la semana.

—

English: I live near my sister and cousin, so we meet for coffee every week.

Spanish: Vivo cerca de mi hermana y primo, por lo que nos vemos cada semana para tomar café.

—

English: I look like my older sister.

Spanish: Me parezco a mi hermana mayor.

—

English: My brother takes after my mother in the face he gets when he is confused about something.

Spanish: Mi hermano se parece a mi madre en la cara que pone cuando está confundido por algo.

—

English: Thick curly hair runs in my family

Spanish: El pelo rizado viene de familia.

—

English: He loves football like his dad

Spanish: Le encanta el futbol igual que su padre.

—

English: What do you and your family like to do?

Spanish: ¿Qué les gusta hacer a tu familia y a ti?

—

English: My siblings, cousins and I have many things in common.

Spanish: Mis hermanos, primos y yo tenemos muchas cosas en común.

—

English: My mom is 45 years old but she looks very young.

Spanish: Mi mamá tiene 45 años pero luce muy joven.

—

English: Although my father gets angry a lot, he has a heart like sugar and everyone knows it.

Spanish: Aunque mi padre se enoja mucho, tiene un corazón dulce y todo el mundo lo sabe.

—

English: My sister is starting school today, we are all very excited.

Spanish: Mi hermana empieza la escuela hoy, estamos todos muy emocionados.

—

English: The school principal punished him for fighting at school yesterday.

Spanish: El director de la escuela lo castigó por pelear en la escuela ayer.

—

English: I have two brothers and a sister, I love them all.

Spanish: Tengo dos hermanos y una hermana, los amo a todos.

—

English: My sister is going to the university this year, we are all very happy.

Spanish: Mi hermana va a la universidad este año, estamos todos muy felices.

—

English: My aunt lives abroad, so we can't meet her very often.

Spanish: Mi tía vive en el extranjero, por lo que no podemos verla muy a menudo.

—

English: My father always advises my brothers and me.

Spanish: Mi padre siempre nos aconseja a mis hermanos y a mí.

—

English: We get along very well with all my cousins and have a great time.

Spanish: Nos llevamos muy bien con todos mis primos y lo pasamos muy bien.

—

English: We made chocolate cake with my little sister today.

Spanish: Hicimos pastel de chocolate con mi hermana pequeña hoy.

—

English: My brother will be back from Germany tonight, we will all wait for him at the airport.

Spanish: Mi hermano regresará esta noche de Alemania, todos lo esperaremos en el aeropuerto.

—

English: Jack's wife is going on vacation today.

Spanish: La esposa de Jack se va de vacaciones.

—

English: My little niece has her birthday today.

Spanish: Mi pequeña sobrina cumple años hoy.

—

English: I saw her husband going to work today, we met in the morning.

Spanish: Hoy vi a su esposo ir a trabajar, nos encontramos por la mañana.

—

English: My uncle's children studied abroad and they speak English very well.

Spanish: Los hijos de mi tío estudiaron en el extranjero y hablan muy bien el inglés.

—

English: While looking at our old photos on the computer, we also saw pictures of my deceased grandfather.

Spanish: Mientras miramos nuestras fotos antiguas en la computadora, también vimos fotos de mi abuelo fallecido.

—

English: My nephew went to the dentist this morning because his tooth ached.

Spanish: Mi sobrino fue al dentista esta mañana porque le dolía el diente.

—

English: My father and uncle will come by car in 5 minutes.

Spanish: Mi padre y mi tío vendrán en coche en 5 minutos.

—

English: We went to the market with my mother, we met my aunts.

Spanish: Fuimos al mercado con mi madre, conocimos a mis tías.

—

English: My aunt and her children are coming to dinner today.

Spanish: Mi tía y sus hijos vendrán a cenar hoy.

—

English: My mom invited our whole family to dinner today, and I am sure she made very good food.

Spanish: Mi mamá invitó a toda la familia a cenar hoy, y estoy seguro de que preparó muy buena comida.

—

English: This beautiful white cat has become a new member of our family, we all love it very much.

Spanish: Este hermoso gato blanco se ha convertido en un nuevo miembro de nuestra familia, todos lo amamos mucho.

—

English: My uncle had a fight with my father last year.

Spanish: Mi tío se peleó con mi padre el año pasado.

—

English: They never got along.

Spanish: Nunca se llevaron bien.

—

English: My grandmother has been living alone for about 10 years, she will be moving to our home now.

Spanish: Mi abuela ha estado viviendo sola durante unos 10 años, ahora se mudará a nuestra casa.

—

English: Our father-in-law gave us a share of inheritance.

Spanish: Nuestro suegro nos dio una parte de la herencia.

—

English: My grandfather is building a new house in the village this year.

Spanish: Mi abuelo está construyendo una nueva casa en el pueblo este año.

—

English: My wife will cook for us today.

Spanish: Mi esposa cocinará para nosotros hoy.

—

English: My uncle came back from the village today and said that he would stop by the evening and leave the food he brought from the village.

Spanish: Mi tío regresó hoy del pueblo y dijo que pasaría por la noche y dejaría la comida que trajo del pueblo.

—

English: I brought good news from your son.

Spanish: Traje buenas noticias de tu hijo.

—

English: We met your daughter this morning.

Spanish: Conocimos a tu hija esta mañana.

—

English: The husband's sister has three children.

Spanish: La hermana del marido tiene tres hijos.

—

English: Today we are planning to take the children and go to a picnic.

Spanish: Hoy planeamos llevar a los niños e ir a un picnic.

—

English: My grandfather and grandmother are going on vacation today.

Spanish: Mi abuelo y mi abuela se van de vacaciones hoy.

—

English: I came from far away to see my grandparents, so I'm so tired.

Spanish: Vine de lejos para ver a mis abuelos, así que estoy muy cansado.

—

English: My brother is a computer engineer and understands everything about computer.

Spanish: Mi hermano es ingeniero informático y entiende todo de las computadoras.

—

English: My mother just called me because she missed me so much and we talked for a long time.

Spanish: Mi madre me acaba de llamar porque me extrañaba mucho y hablamos durante mucho tiempo.

—

English: My sister and brother played without leaving the pool from morning to evening.

Spanish: Mi hermana y mi hermano jugaban sin salir de la piscina desde la mañana hasta la noche.

—

English: My niece gave birth this morning so we will go to the hospital together.

Spanish: Mi sobrina dio a luz esta mañana, así que iremos juntas al hospital.

—

English: I thought you didn't have any family.

Spanish: Pensé que no tenías familia.

—

English: I usually eat at home with my family.

Spanish: Normalmente como en casa con mi familia.

—

English: My mother gets up the earliest in my family.

Spanish: Mi madre se levanta más temprano en mi familia.

—

English: My family was well off in those days.

Spanish: Mi familia estaba bien en esos días.

—

English: Her husband is an engineer.

Spanish: Su esposo es ingeniero.

—

English: My wife is a housewife.

Spanish: Mi esposa es ama de casa.

—

English: Their parents are strict.

Spanish: Sus padres son estrictos.

—

English: My mom is very intelligent.

Spanish: Mi mamá es muy inteligente.

—

English: Her father is very practical.

Spanish: Su papá es muy práctico.

—

English: Nuestra hija es linda.

Spanish: Our daughter is beautiful.

—

English: Our son is creative.

Spanish: Nuestro hijo es creativo.

—

English: Su hermano es doctor.

Spanish: Her brother is a doctor.

—

English: Her sister is a nurse.

Spanish: Su hermana es enfermera.

—

English: Nuestros abuelos están casados.

Spanish: Our grandparents are married.

—

English: My grandfather is an energetic old man.

Spanish: Mi abuelo es un anciano my enérgico.

—

English: My grandmother is very affectionate.

Spanish: Mi abuela es muy cariñosa.

—

English: Her grandchildren are naughty.

Spanish: Sus nietos son traviesos.

—

English: His grandchildren is still a baby.

Spanish: Su nieto es todavía un bebé.

—

English: My granddaughter is very beautiful.

Spanish: Mi nieta es muy bonita.

—

English: My uncles and aunts are very fun.

Spanish: Mis tíos son muy divertidos.

—

English: Maria's children are adorable.

Spanish: Los hijos de María son adorables.

—

English: Our step-mother is good

Spanish: Nuestra madrastra es buena.

—

English: My mother in law is angry

Spanish: Mi suegra esta enojada.

—

STORY-TIME Chapter 12: Pumpkin Ice cream (English)

Mom: When I was young my favourite ice cream flavor was chocolate.

Dad: Really honey? I don't like chocolate. I think chocolate is overrated.

Son: I don't agree dad. I think chocolate is the glory.

Mom: Yeah, you are right. Your dad is crazy.

Dad: Honey! My favourite flavor of ice cream is pumpkin.

Son: What? That's horrible!

Mom: I think the same.

Dad: Definitely you are boring.

Son: Dad we are smart not boring.

Mom: Yeah baby. Your father is a bit peculiar.

Dad: I am an interesting person.

Son: I don't think that. I think you are an alien.

STORY-TIME Capítulo 12: Helado de calabaza (Español)

Mamá: Cuando era joven mi helado favorito era el de chocolate

Papá: ¿De verdad cariño? No me gusta el chocolate. Creo que el chocolate está sobrevalorado.

Hijo: No estoy de acuerdo papá. Creo que el chocolate es la gloria.

Mamá: Así es mi bebé, tienes razón. Tu papá está loco.

Papá: ¡Cariño! Mi sabor favorito de helado es de calabaza

Son: ¿Qué? ¡Eso es horrible!

Mamá: Pienso lo mismo

Dad: Definitivamente ustedes son aburridos

Hijo: Papá, somos inteligentes no aburridos

Mamá: Sí hijito, tu papá es un poco peculiar

Papá: Soy una persona interesante

Hijo: No lo creo. Pienso que eres un alienígena

———

CHAPTER TWELVE TEST.

1. Who's the mother of your mother?
A Mi abuela
B Mi sobrina
C Mi abuelo
D Mi hijo

2. What does "Married" means?
A Concubino
B Soltero
C Divorciado
D Casado

3. How do you say "Uncle" in spanish?
A Primo
B Hija
C Tío
D Novio

4. How do you say "godfather" in spanish?
A Papá bueno
B Padrino
C Madrina
D Padrastro

5. What word means "Mother-in-law"
A Madrastra
B Padrastro
C Suegra
D Mamá legal

Answers: 1) A, 2) D, 3) C, 4) B, 5) C.